IMMIGRANT INTEGRATION
AND
URBAN RENEWAL IN TORONTO

by

BRIGITTE NEUMANN,

RICHARD MEZOFF

and

ANTHONY H. RICHMOND

MARTINUS NIJHOFF
THE HAGUE
1973

ISBN 90 247 1308 0

PRINTED IN BELGIUM

ACKNOWLEDGEMENTS

The research on which this report is based was carried out with the assistance of research grants from York University, the Canada Council, the Central Mortgage and Housing Corporation of Canada, Ottawa, and Denison Mines Ltd. The authors wish to express their appreciation to these agencies and to their colleagues and assistants in the Ethnic Research Programme of the Institute for Behavioural Research at York University for their help. In particular, thanks are due to the Director, Dr. C. Michael Lanphier and staff of the Survey Research Centre of York University who carried out the sample survey, together with Mrs. Nilly Akerman, Mrs. Diane Erickson and Mrs. Karen Kaplan who provided valuable help with the programming and data analysis.

This book has been published with the help of a grant from the Social Sciences Research Council of Canada using funds provided by the Canada Council.

TABLE OF CONTENTS

LIST OF TABLES

INTRODUCTION :
IMMIGRATION AND URBAN RENEWAL POLICIES

The urban renewal study conducted for the Metropolitan Toronto Planning Board and published in August, 1966, stated that Toronto lacked many of the social and economic problems of metropolitan areas in the United States. Particularly, the report states "there are no concentrations of disadvantaged minority racial groups and relatively little social segregation." (Metropolitan Toronto Planning Board, 1966: ii). Even if the term "racial" in this statement is interpreted literally, the statement is not entirely accurate. It overlooks the position of the Asian, particularly Chinese, population resident in the downtown area. This population has already been partially displaced by the clearance preparatory to the building of the new City Hall and is further threatened by other proposed developments in that vicinity. It is true that Toronto does not have a Negro ghetto comparable with those found in American cities such as Detroit, Chicago, New York, etc. although there are distinct clusters of non-whites. However, if the term "ethnic" is substituted for "racial" the evidence shows that there is a substantial degree of ethnic segregation in certain areas, and this tends to coincide in some localities with indices of social and economic deprivation. High concentrations of particular ethnic minorities in certain areas of the city are correlated with low education, low income, high unemployment, multiple occupation and overcrowding and, to a lesser extent, with the incidence of "blight" in its various forms. (Richmond, 1967:12; Murdie, 1969.)

In many cases these ethnic neighbourhoods are made up of close-knit networks of kith and kin that have been built up on the basis of refugee movements or sponsored immigration. A large proportion of the population has only a limited knowledge of

English and the community functions on the basis of a variety of ethnic institutions that operate in the immigrant's own mother tongue. These include local stores and markets, churches, clubs, welfare agencies and other organizations that serve the needs of the local population. Frequently employment opportunities in occupations where English is unnecessary are also available to men and women in the neighbourhood. These ethnic neighbourhoods exhibit a high degree of functional interdependence which would be severely disrupted by urban renewal schemes involving widespread clearance. The proposed extension of freeways could give rise to problems in this respect. Even the "spot clearance" schemes of a more limited kind would have more serious social and human repercussions in such areas in view of the high incidence of "doubling".

It is significant that certain planning areas in which urban renewal has already proceeded, such as the Don area including the Regent Park public housing scheme, have consisted predominantly of native-born Canadians of British origin. The experience gained in these schemes is not likely to be a useful guide to the probable consequences of improvement and other schemes in those areas with a more heterogeneous population. An examination of the population characteristics in those areas designated for renewal in the future suggests that the social effects and human implications of these plans may be somewhat different from past experience. The report of the Metropolitan Toronto Planning Board, 1966, designated 8 renewal districts. Two of these ("A" and "H") are outside the boundaries of the City of Toronto. (See map, p. 7)

Urban Renewal Policies

In the past five years there has been a radical change in the official approach to urban renewal in Toronto. Experience here, as in other North American cities, confirms that urban renewal schemes drawn up by planning authorities without consultation with the inhabitants of the area affected are likely to arouse considerable opposition. (Canadian Welfare Council, 1968; Gans, 1962: 305-335). However well intentioned, such plans are frequently perceived as a threat to property owners and tenants alike. The former fear that compensation will be inadequate in the event of their property being subject to compulsory purchase. Tenants, in their turn, fear that alternative accommodation of a suitable kind in a convenient locality at a price they can afford will not be available. The experience of the Toronto City Planning Authorities, particularly in connection with the Trefann Court urban renewal scheme, has convinced them of the necessity of consultation with property owners and residents in the area concerned, before proceeding with an urban renewal scheme. The City has deliberately encouraged the participation of residents' committees in the planning process through the formation of a *local* planning council. Such a council is usually composed of (a) representatives of the Residents' Association; (b) representatives of local business; (c) local Aldermen; (d) planner in charge of the area; (e) representative of the building inspection office; (f) any other representation of relevant groups.

The renewal districts described in the report are probably best regarded as "primary planning units," since there is no intention to undertake immediate or extensive clearance. Instead, a gradual process of rehabilitation and renewal is envisaged. It is important to note that, in 1961, the populations of the eight renewal districts or primary planning units differed essentially from each other and from those areas in which urban renewal has already been undertaken in Toronto. The very high proportions of foreign-born and others whose mother tongue was not English in areas such as Kensington and Gore Vale, together with the close knit ties of family and kinship characteristic of these neighbourhoods, will almost certainly influence attitudes towards urban renewal.

Although ethnic segregation is not confined to the central city areas, as is shown in other research reports (Darroch and Marston, 1969; Richmond, 1972), there is no doubt that it is an important feature of the central districts of Toronto, including those eventually designated for renewal. Research in a comparable area of Hamilton has drawn attention to the high frequency and importance of primary group relations with friends and neighbours in a working-class area with a large proportion of foreign-born. (Pineo, 1968). At the same time it is important to note that the foreign-born families are not necessarily over-represented in the most seriously dilapidated "pockets" of poor housing.

A further significant development in the philosophy of urban renewal has been the increasing emphasis upon rehabilitation of existing property, rather than wholesale clearance and redevelopment. Unlike some North American cities, Toronto does not have a very large area of 19th century development that cannot be brought up to modern standards of amenity. On the contrary, although much of the housing in the urban renewal areas is subject to urban blight of various kinds and frequently lacks adequate amenities, it is frequently structurally sound and capable of an extended lease of life. Given the shortage of housing, the high cost of demolition and redevelopment and the urgent need for low cost housing, rehabilitation appears to offer better prospects than any alternative approach.

However, the emphasis upon rehabilitation could have two unanticipated consequences, which would be significant in relation to immigration and the formation and maintenance of ethnic communities. Firstly, the encouragement of private initiative in rehabilitating older property in the downtown areas may have the effect of encouraging middle-class people to invest in the properties and to subsequently occupy them at lower densities than formerly. The current vogue for "town houses" is an illustration of this process. The investment necessary to raise the amenity to the middle-class level of expectation is such that their subsequent sale price or rental will be beyond the means of the majority of working-class people, irrespective of ethnic origin. From the point of view of the local municipality, such rehabilitation has the advantage of raising the taxable capacity of the area. However, it also has the effect of "exporting" the poorer sections of the population to other neighbourhoods.

The second consequence of encouraging local initiative in rehabilitation, particularly when associated with the formation of residents' associations who negotiate with the planning authorities for the renewal of the area concerned, is to reduce the mobility of the population. Given the overall shortage of housing, the high cost of housing in the suburban areas, and the desire of people living in a particular locality to improve their housing conditions, the possibility of local improvement is an attractive one. It is a means of improving the material conditions and social position without the necessity of breaking the ties that have been established with the local community. When neighbourhoods of this kind have a high proportion of a given ethnic group it may be a means by which a transient reception area is converted into an ethnic community with a firm ecological basis.

If an area which has formerly served as an immigrant reception area is subsequently converted into an ethnic community with strong local roots and vested interests in the maintenance of social institutions and the preservation of property rights acquired in the area, this means that subsequent waves of immigrants may have even greater difficulty in finding suitable housing at a price that they can afford. Under certain conditions, a process of "filtering down" may result in other areas becoming transient reception areas in their turn. However, zoning bylaws, the maintenance of housing standards bylaws and the encouragement of local effort to maintain and rehabilitate existing housing throughout the city may inhibit this process and further increase the scarcity of suitable low cost housing. Officials of the City Planning Authority admit that the special needs of immigrants are not taken into account in urban renewal plans. In a city such as Toronto which receives such a large number of immigrants annually, the neglect of such considerations is surprising. The functions once performed and the needs met by unplanned transient reception areas may have to be deliberately anticipated and provided for in the future, as part of the urban planning process.

In the following chapters some of the questions raised above will be considered in more detail, beginning with an examination of the areas designated by the Metropolitan Toronto Planning Board as potential urban renewal areas and their condition. These areas are those in which the survey was conducted in 1969; the methods used in the selection of the sample and in the analysis of the data are then described. The demographic, ethnic and socio-economic characteristics of the householders are examined, followed by a consideration of attitudes to urban renewal and their determinants. This is followed by a detailed consideration of factors associated with participation in voluntary organizations, both as an indicator of social integration and because of the practical importance of this question as it affects 'citizen participation' in the planning process. Finally, in the conclusion, some geographic and ethnic variations within the survey areas are noted and the implications of the findings as a whole for urban renewal and immigrant integration considered.

I

LONG-TERM PLANS FOR URBAN IMPROVEMENT IN TORONTO

In 1966, the Metropolitan Toronto Planning Board published the results of an extensive study of the physical and structural conditions of individual dwellings and areas in Toronto. The objective of the study was to identify physically blighted or substandard occupied areas which would require government intervention if improvement was to be achieved. The study included residential, commercial, and industrial dwellings. The report indicated that Metropolitan Toronto possesses no serious concentration of residential or non-residential blight; but, rather, a widespread distribution of a moderate degree of blight.[1] As might be expected, older areas were judged to be more seriously blighted than newer areas. One hundred and forty blocks were considered to have over one-half of their dwellings in bad or poor structural condition. Two hundred more blocks were reported to have one-fifth to one-half of their dwellings in bad or poor condition. Additionally, there were indications of a serious shortage of suitable housing available for families with low or moderate income. As a consequence, there is a rather high rate of involuntary "doubling up" of families, as will be shown below.

[1] A building is considered blighted if there is any substantial impairment of the building's ability to perform its intended function. Thus blight included conditions not only of structural inadequacy, but of conditions of obsolescence in terms of carrying out its intended function. A building was rated as deteriorated if there were major structural deficiencies such as leaning walls, a sagging roof, or cracked foundations. A building possessing any of these deficiencies was rated as being in poor condition, a building with lesser deficiencies was rated as being in bad condition, a building without apparent deficiencies of this type was rated as sound.

In terms of the structural condition of dwellings findings were similar for the commercial districts of Toronto; there was a widespread occurrence of moderate degrees of physical blight, but few dwellings were reported to have undergone serious deterioration. Only one and one-half percent of the 22,500 commercial buildings in Toronto were rated as being seriously deteriorated. The most pressing problem for commercial dwellings was, rather, that of functional blight or the obsolescence of a site. Commercial obsolescence is the result of changes in retailing procedures which render the location, size, or physical layout of an existing store inefficient for its present use. These conditions in turn create high vacancy rates, and thus a high incidence of patterns of inefficient land use in present commercial districts.

Industrial obsolescence in Metropolitan Toronto has been the product of many of the same forces as the above-mentioned commercial obsolescence; changes in age, design, and function. In the case of industries, however, there is the added factor that the industry is often not only blighted, but also has a blighting effect on the remainder of the neighbourhood. Five hundred Toronto industries were regarded as being either blighted themselves, or as having blighting effects on their neighbourhood. Many of these industries are located in otherwise residential neighbourhoods, and thus prevent the use of adjacent land sites for any type of use. Many industries have thus become problematic because they have precluded an economically more efficient use of land in an industrial or commercial neighbourhood, or have prevented what may be regarded as a more desirable use of neighbouring land in residential areas. As will be seen below, this type of incompatible land use has been an important factor in the determination of the nature of the proposed urban renewal programme.

Industrial blight was relatively concentrated in two distinct geographic bands; one extending west from the downtown area along the main-line railway corridor into the "Junction" area, the other extending east from downtown along the main-line railway corridor and into East York and Scarborough. One further area, in the Southern Etobicoke and Lakeshore suburbs about eight miles from down-town, possesses similar characteristics, but as will be shown below, was excluded from our sampling population because it is not within the limits of the city of Toronto.

Finally, the Planning Board reported that Toronto, in contrast to most American cities of comparable size, is not characterized by a widespread pattern of residential and social segregation of disadvantaged racial minority groups. Rather, residential neighbourhoods were viewed for the most part as stable areas, representing wide cross-sections of the population, and generating satisfactory levels of economic activity. However, as has been noted in the introduction to this report, the substitution of the word "ethnic" for "racial" leads to some modification of this view. Residential segregation for ethnic minority groups, notably the Jews, Italians, and Russians, is quite high; and patterns of segregation between various ethnic groups are also present (Darroch and Marston, 1969). It is interesting to note that in some cases ethnic areas or neighbourhoods correspond quite closely to areas of the city which were subsequently designated as prospective urban renewal areas.

On the basis of the general findings noted above, and the more specific conditions observed in individual areas, a long-term urban renewal programme for Metropolitan Toronto was developed. The programme, intended to be implemented over a fifteen-year period had four broadly-stated objectives, which were:

1. The improvement of deteriorated residential neighbourhoods through public and private activities involving the clearance or rehabilitation of deteriorated properties, the maintenance of suitable housing standards, removal of incompatible land usages, and provision of a variety of public improvements and services to residential areas;

2. The provision of housing accommodation for families with low or moderate incomes;

3. The reorganization and improvement of older industrial areas to facilitate operation of existing industries, and the provision of space for industries displaced from residential neighbourhoods;

4. The reorganization and improvement of viable commercial districts in older sections of the Metropolitan area, and rational re-use of marginal commercial land.

More specifically, it involves a set of recommendations for the types of renewal treatment to be applied, as well as the determining criteria for deciding whether or not public renewal is necessary.

In general, private renewal is always given first priority, and public intervention occurs only where private programmes have not been implemented and are not expected to be implemented.

Four types of renewal treatments were proposed for various dwellings and areas: residential clearance, residential spot clearance, industrial spot clearance, and industrial maintenance and rehabilitation. A fifth designation, that of special treatment area, indicates that the exact treatment and usage of the site have not been completely determined.

In the planning of the operational stages of renewal, the Planning Board designated eight small sectors as "First Priority Sectors," intending that these sectors be the first to undergo the proposed urban renewal treatments. Theoretically, these sectors were given priority because they would afford Toronto the opportunity to provide the maximum net gain in housing accommodation. However, total housing requirements of those to be displaced by renewal in these sectors will probably exceed the total housing supply which Toronto will be able to offer in these sectors.

These priority areas contain almost fifteen thousand dwellings, or just under thirty percent of the total dwellings chosen for urban renewal. Apparently, there are no significant differences between priority sectors and the remainder of the urban renewal areas in terms of the structural conditions of the dwellings. Fully eighty percent of the dwellings are in sound structural condition, with about twenty percent in poor or bad condition in each case. In terms of proposed treatments, in both instances, the majority will undergo residential spot clearance. The priority areas will undergo a slightly higher percentage of residential clearance, 3.6 % to 1.8 %, and possess slightly fewer special areas with undetermined treatment, 1.7 % to 3.0 %. This probably indicates a desire on the part of the planners to minimize treatment of areas or dwellings on which the most beneficial use has yet to be determined.

The Development of Metropolitan Toronto

The major problem of urban renewal, as defined by the Planning Board, was that of meeting and eliminating obsolescent features of the urban community. A major objective of urban renewal, under this scheme, is to adjust the obsolete parts of the urban community so that they fit the needs of the present and the future. Thus, aside from studying the structural conditions of dwellings and businesses, the patterns of growth and requirements of the Toronto metropolis must be taken into account when a programme for urban renewal is formulated. Because of this, a look at the recent past and near future development of Toronto is in order.

Metropolitan Toronto, encompassing 240 square miles, had an estimated population of 1,850,000 in 1966. About eighty percent of the total land area had been developed, and virtually all of this area is expected to be developed by 1975. At that time, the population of Metropolitan Toronto is expected to be between two and one-half and three million. Metropolitan Toronto itself is the result of a federation of the City of Toronto and its twelve immediate suburbs into one centralized metropolitan system, comprising six interdependent municipalities.

Toronto has exhibited a growth rate of twenty percent annually in recent years. It appears that natural population increase, and net gains due to migration have contributed about equally to this growth. Migration to Toronto has come both from other areas of Canada, and from other nations. In 1971, half of the householders of Toronto had been born outside Canada.

It is important for the purposes of this study to distinguish between the patterns of development of the inner-city area, and the suburban areas of Toronto. There are important differences between these areas in terms of population growth, population characteristics, and labour and employment market characteristics.

Despite the rapid growth of Metropolitan Toronto as a whole, the population of the City of Toronto itself has remained almost constant for the twelve years prior to the issue of the Planning Board's report. During this same twelve-year period, the outer suburbs of North York, Etobicoke, and Scarborough more than tripled in population, and the population of the inner suburbs grew by twenty-five percent. The outer suburbs now hold forty-six percent of the population of Metropolitan Toronto, as opposed to thirty-six percent in the city itself. Ultimately, about sixty percent of the population is expected to live in the outer suburbs.

Paralleling the rise in proportion of people living in the suburbs is the rise in proportion of people living in apartment houses. Apartments made up ten percent of all Toronto housing in 1951, twenty percent in 1961 and twenty-five percent in 1966. From 1960 until 1966, fifty-five percent of all new housing constructed was apartment housing.

Finally, two further facts should be noted. First, forty-four percent of the population of Metropolitan Toronto is in the labour force, which represents a relatively high non-dependent population proportion. One-half of these workers are white-collar or non-manual workers, the majority being employed in manufacturing, but growing numbers are being employed in commerce and finance as Toronto assumes more importance as a national centre in these spheres of trade. Here again the population is not uniform in distribution, however, with forty-five percent of inner-city dwellers being white-collar workers, fifty percent of inner-suburb dwellers being white-collars, and sixty percent of the population residing in the outer suburbs being white-collar workers.

Second, the inner-city area at present provides sixty percent of the metropolis' employment, whereas it provided fifty percent in 1950. Thus, in Toronto as in most North American cities, there is a clear pattern of the inner-city becoming an area where people come only for employment, and, in increasing numbers move their residences to the suburbs. Despite these trends, it was interesting to note that the Planning Board did not consider it necessary to reverse the trend of suburban exodus by the non-dependent population, or to substantially revise existing land-use patterns.

The Urban Renewal Areas of Toronto

Six areas within the city of Toronto have been designated as prospective "urban renewal areas." Due to the negative connotation the term "urban renewal" has acquired these would now be better described as potential improvement areas.

These six areas, containing just over fifty thousand dwellings expected to undergo renewal treatment, were labelled as Areas B-G. Two other areas, labelled A and H, are within the boundaries of Metropolitan Toronto, but are not within the city of Toronto, and thus are not included in our sample.

Area B, known as the "Junction area," contains the "Toronto Diamond" railway interchange, and is bounded by the CNR tracks and the Keele/St. Clair stockyards on two sides, and by Bloor St.

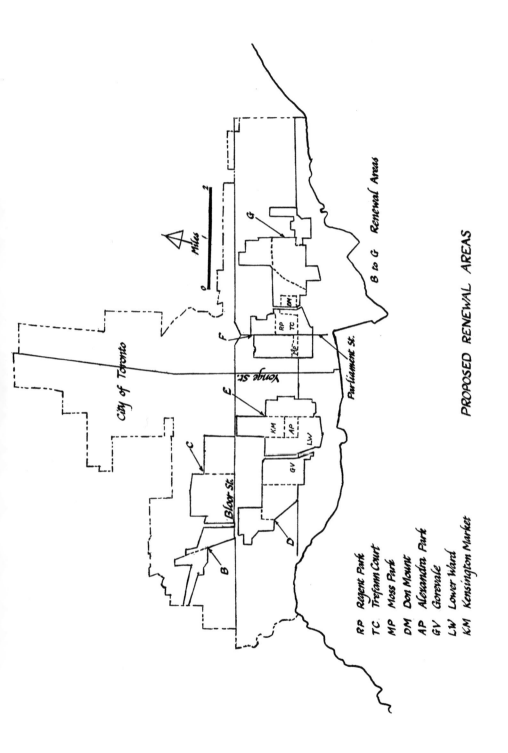

PROPOSED RENEWAL AREAS

RP   Regent Park
T.C. Trefann Court
MP   Moss Park
DM   Don Mount
AP   Alexandra Park
GV   Gorevale
LW   Lower Ward
KM   Kensington Market

B to G   Renewal Areas

on the south. Almost four thousand dwellings in this area are scheduled for urban renewal treatment, eighty percent of which will undergo residential spot clearance. A major cause of deterioration in this area has been the penetration of many industries into otherwise residential areas. This factor, combined with the blighting effects of the stockyards and the railways have limited the amount of private rehabilitation which has been undertaken. Thus, there is the perception of the need for publicly coordinated urban renewal activities.

Area C, a large district containing almost ten thousand dwelling units scheduled for renewal treatment, is predominantly residential with the exception of the westernmost sector extending along the CNR tracks. While residential blight has been found in only seven percent of the dwellings in this area, many more dwellings are vulnerable due to the presence of nearby blighting industries. Further, it is intended that the extension of a major expressway pass through what is now the northernmost boundary of this area. A major objective of the renewal programme in this area is the removal of blighting industries from otherwise residential neighbourhoods.

Area D, lying between the CNR/CPR lines and proposed extension of a major expressway, contains a high proportion of non-residential blight. Almost one-fourth of all housing in this area is considered to be deteriorated. Included in this area is one sector in which a large amount of complete residential clearance is anticipated.

Area E, between Bloor and Queen Streets, and extending east from Grace St. to University Ave., contains over eleven-thousand prospective renewal dwellings almost thirty-five percent of which are deteriorated. It is characterized by the existence of extensive patterns of incompatible land uses, and by many blighted or blighting non-residential sites. Sidewalks are in poor repair throughout this area, and off-street parking is considered to be inadequate. A major objective of the renewal programme in this area is the separation of residential and industrial neighbourhoods.

Area F, east of the downtown area, lying between Jarvis St. and the Don River, includes the area where most of Toronto's past urban renewal activities have taken place. Excluding areas of recently built public housing, almost forty percent of the housing in this area is considered deteriorated, with most housing south of Queen St. considered to be deteriorated.

Area G, extending from the Don River to Coxwell Ave., and bounded by Danforth Ave. on the north, includes the site of the Don Mount renewal area, a recent Toronto urban renewal project. This area contains almost eleven thousand dwellings scheduled to be treated, almost eighty percent of which will undergo residential spot clearance. Many blocks in this area are vulnerable to pollution from nearby blighting industries, including a hydro plant, a sewage disposal plant, and municipal incinerator. A shortage of rehousing facilities in this area for families displaced by residential clearance is anticipated.

It is important that our analysis of the urban renewal areas examines not only the characteristics of dwelling conditions within the areas, but the social characteristics as well. Examination of the data presented in the Planning Board's Report of 1966 makes visible various patterns of social characteristics of the inhabitants of these areas. All six areas showed greater percentages of overcrowded dwellings than the remainder of the city. The urban renewal areas as a whole exhibited a lower incidence of tenant-occupied dwellings than the remainder of the city, although two areas, E and F did not follow this general pattern. The foreign-born population of Toronto seemed to be concentrated more closely in these areas than in the remainder of the City of Toronto, although areas F and G had lower proportions of post-war immigrants, and area B had approximately the same proportion, twenty-nine percent, as opposed to twenty-seven percent in the remainder of the city. The renewal areas also possessed higher proportions of large families (five or more children), and families taking in lodgers than in the remainder of the city, although once again, there are variations within individual areas. Finally, the renewal areas as a whole exhibited rather similar rates of geographic mobility to the remainder of the city. The only substantial variation occurred in area F, which had thirty-three percent of its population composed of residents of less than one year's duration.

Unfortunately, the Planning Board's study failed to examine the attitude of the residents in these areas toward urban renewal as it might affect them. This study was designed in part to make up this deficiency.

II

SURVEY METHODOLOGY

The interviews on which this report is based were conducted in the City of Toronto, specifically in those sections designated as long-range urban-renewal areas by the Metropolitan Planning Board in their 1966 study.

Construction of Interview Schedule and Fieldwork

One of the major concerns of the investigators during formation of the interview schedule arose from the expectation that the respondents would tend to have a relatively low level of education and that, for a large proportion of the respondents, English would be a second language. In addition, some of the topics covered in the interview, such as housing policy, required a good deal of familiarity with current events and a certain level of awareness of urban problems. In order to avoid a high rate of non-response or many responses based on misunderstanding, one of the investigators' continuous goals was to phrase questions as simply and as clearly as possible.

Before the interview schedule was used in the field, the Survey Research Centre of York University conducted a pre-test of the first draft in Ottawa. The neighbourhood in which the pre-testing was carried out was similar to the areas of our concern. The pre-test interviewers were instructed to interview especially foreign-born respondents with language difficulties in order to point out areas of the interview schedule which would be particularly problematic.

The inspection of pre-test results demonstrated, first and foremost, that the interview was too long. As a result, sections on acculturation, on political activity and on ethnic prejudice were either eliminated or shortened. Many other questions were re-aranged and formulated in simpler terms.

Before the interview schedule was finalized, it was once again tested to ensure that it was not too long and that the questions were acceptable to the respondents. Past experience had demonstrated that interviews should not be much longer than one hour; in longer interviews, respondent and interviewer fatigue presents special problems about validity and reliability of data obtained toward the end of the interview.

The fieldwork finally began during the last week of May, 1969, and continued to the beginning of July, 1969. The interviewers were trained to select respondents (see selection criteria below) and were also trained to administer the interview schedules. Because there is a high proportion of foreign-born in the districts we surveyed, a number of foreign-language interviewers were used: on the interviewing staff were people who spoke Italian, Portugese, Ukrainian, Polish, Czech, and Chinese. The procedure adopted was that if an interviewer was unable to interview a respondent because of language problems, another interviewer who could speak the required language was sent to complete the interview.

A letter explaining the study was sent out to the selected addresses by the Survey Research Centre. When a selected person refused to be interviewed, a second letter was sent out, emphasizing the importance of the selected person's participation. Then, another interviewer approached the selected person for an interview. Table 1 indicates response rates for the survey. Seventy-two percent of the contacts resulted in completed interviews; the refusal rate was eleven percent; other reasons accounted for the remaining seventeen per cent. There were, then, 316 completed interviews.

TABLE 1. *Response Rates*

Result of Contact	N	%
Completed Interview	316	72
Dead Addresses	20	4
I11/Senile	14	3
Refusals	49	11
Absent	32	7
Other	9	3
Total Number of Contacts	440	100

Selection of Respondents and Sample Design

The respondents for this study were heads of families in the urban renewal areas. Certain parts of the urban renewal areas were, however, eliminated from the population from which the sample was drawn.

First, all public housing developments were eliminated, because many of the inhabitants had moved from neighbourhoods previously subject to clearance. On the other hand, the probability of selecting a number of public housing residents sufficient to make their separate analysis meaningful was very low.

Secondly, all institutions such as hospitals or old-age homes were left out. As above, the scope of this relatively small study did not extend to these special sub-categories of the population of urban renewal areas.

Finally, only addresses containing households were listed. For example, stores or other businesses were not listed unless someone actually resided there.

The task of the interviewer in selecting a respondent involved three stages: first, distinguishing households within addresses; secondly, distinguishing families within households; finally, if there was more than one family, selecting one of the male heads of family by means of a randomized selection table. Definitions of household and family allowed the interviewer to make the selection. Special rules were devised for non-family households, such as boarding-houses or unrelated persons sharing an apartment.

A household was defined as a group of persons who share a dwelling and usually eat their meals together. If a household did not contain any families, as defined below, the selected person for the interview was the head of the household; that is, the person so designated by the group, or the person who was in charge of the household (such as the landlord in a rooming-house), or the person who paid household bills such as the rent.

The definition for a family is highly similar to the one used in the Census. The family was defined as a husband and wife (with or without children) or a parent with children. The children were considered part of the parents' family if they had never been married. Married children in the household or anyone else in the household, related or unrelated, to the head of the household, were families if their spouse and/or children also lived there. If the husband or father was present, he was the head of the family. Otherwise, the wife or mother was the head. If the head of the family was female, she was not eligible for selection unless this family was the only one in the household.

Obviously, what is ordinarily defined as the head of the household and the head of the family frequently coincided. Our original intention following this difficult selection procedure was to distinguish "doubled-up" families and to analyze them separately. In fact, the relatively crowded downtown areas are not characterized by a break-down of nuclear family patterns and the widespread occurrence of multiple-family households. In our sample, there were only fourteen instances of this arrangement. On the other hand, multiple-household dwellings as opposed to multiple-family households were common. Some were lodging houses catering for single males and transients but the majority were cases of dwellings divided and rented as separate flats with common entrance.

The sample size desired was approximately three hundred. To allow for refusal rates, approximately four hundred households were to be selected. To save fieldwork, particularly listing costs, a clustered, multi-stage sample was necessary. The final decision was to draw one hundred blocks and out of each block to select approximately four addresses.

At first, it was thought a multi-stage clustered sample would be adequate. That is, at the first sampling stage, blocks would be selected with probability of selection proportional to the household count of each block. Subsequently addresses within blocks would be selected.

Then it came to the attention of the investigators that areas within which urban renewal had been carried out, or within which it was imminent, had already been heavily researched and that such groups as residents' associations were very opposed to further survey research. For that reason it was thought desirable to eliminate the chance of oversampling in those areas by stratification. Three strata were defined; the salience of urban renewal was the criterion used to distinguish them.

In Stratum 1 urban renewal had already occurred; these areas are known as Don Mount (census tract 114) and Alexandra Park (census tract 61). Both Don Mount and Alexandra Park contain public housing, which was not eligible for sampling.

In Stratum 2, urban renewal plans were being made, although little or no urban renewal has occurred: Kensington (census tract 39), Don Vale (census tract 97 and 100), Trefann Court (blocks 18 to 24 of census tract 324) and Victoria Memorial Square (part of census tract 63) are the areas of this type.

Stratum 3 is the rest of the study area. Here urban renewal is a more distant possibility.

Now the first two strata were quite small compared to the third in terms of area; therefore, we realized from the beginning that sample size within the small strata would probably be too small to make separate estimates meaningful. As it turned out, our final sample contained fourteen respondents in Stratum 1, nineteen respondents in Stratum 2, and two hundred and eighty-three respondents in Stratum 3.

However, by the time the decision to stratify had been made, a sample of blocks had already been drawn. Using the technique of post-stratification described by Kish (1965: 90-92) it was found that there would be no heavy concentration of respondents in particularly sensitive areas of the city. After the post-stratification was begun, weights for each stratum were calculated. These weights are "blow-up factors" which are the products of the inverse of the probability of selection of an element at each stage of the selection process. Since the weights were relatively uniform, they were not used in the tables that follow. These weights, modified by corrections for response rate, could be utilized to generate estimates of the population totals.

The sample of blocks was drawn, as mentioned above, with probability of selection proportional to the household count of each block. At the same time a constant yield of four households per block was desired. To compensate for the variability and size of block and allow the constant yield, the following technique was used to keep the probability of selection of addresses equal: if a block was, for example, twice as large as the average block, it had twice the average probability of selection; but, once that block was selected, any addresses within it had half the average probability of selection. In that fashion selection ratios and random starts for each of the one hundred blocks selected in the first sampling stage allowed the selection of addresses in the second sampling stage. The final stage of selecting a respondent within a household has been described above. Since there was almost always only one eligible person, there was no need to allow for varying probabilities with the selection of any particular person within the household.

The final feature of the sample design which will be mentioned here is that the method of replicate sampling was used. This technique is described by Kish (1965: 127-132). Replicate sampling means that our sample can be split into two independent samples from which a coefficient of variation can be calculated as an alternative estimate of sampling error.

Non-Response and Sampling Error

Since no data supplementary to our survey were available for selected persons, it is not possible to assess the effects of non-response on bias.

In the calculation of sampling error, the formula for a simple random sample could not be used because the first stage of the sampling procedure involved the selection of blocks; thus clustering effects must be accounted for. Estimates of sampling error using the formula $2 \sqrt{[p(1-p)/n]}$ probably underestimate the error, as Kish has pointed out. However, the formula $4 \sqrt{[p(1-p)/n]}$ which we have used in the calculation of Table 2 is in all likelihood too conservative. The ranges of error are probably not as large as indicated below.

TABLE 2. *Probable Range of Error at 95% Level of Confidence for Varying Sizes of Sample**

	Percentages								
	$\frac{10}{90}$	$\frac{15}{85}$	$\frac{20}{80}$	$\frac{25}{75}$	$\frac{30}{70}$	$\frac{35}{65}$	$\frac{40}{60}$	$\frac{45}{55}$	$\frac{50}{50}$
Total Sample (N=316)	± 6.7	8.0	9.0	9.7	10.3	10.7	11.0	11.2	11.2
Native-Born (N=120)	±11.0	13.0	14.6	15.8	16.7	17.4	17.9	18.2	18.3
Foreign-Born (N=196)	± 8.6	10.2	11.4	12.4	13.1	13.6	14.0	14.2	14.3

* This table allows for effects of clustering in the sample and is based on the formula $4 \sqrt{[p(1-p)/n]}$ for the sampling error.

Chi-Square was used to test for the significance of relationships throughout this report. Levels of significance appear with each table when applicable and phi or Cramèr's V as a measure of association. Because of the cluster effects in the sample design, differences which do not reach the .01 level of significance should be interpreted with caution.

The Neighbourhood Integration Score

The neighbourhood integration score's composition is specified in Table 3. The items constituting the index were chosen from a larger pool of similar items, on the basis of high inter-item and item-to-total correlations.

TABLE 3. *The Neighbourhood Integration Items*

	Possible Scores for Each Item		
	2	1	0
Satisfaction with neighbourhood	very satisfied	satisfied	other
Feeling at home in neighbourhood	—	yes	no
Satisfaction with house	—	yes	no
House owned or rented	—	owned	rented
Relatives living in neighbourhood	—	yes	no

A distinction between "very satisfied" and "satisfied" was useful only in the case of neighbourhood satisfaction which was scored from zero to two. All other items were scored one or zero. The neighbourhood integration score is the total of the five items scores. Thus the neighbourhood integration score ranges from zero to six.

Participation in Voluntary Associations

Voluntary associations were defined as non-profit, with entry and exit at the free will of the organization and the member, with regular meetings, with some form of structure such as an executive and committees and with specified goals.

Whether churches and trade unions can be included as voluntary associations is somewhat ambiguous. It has been argued that church membership differs from other types because an individual is "born into" a specific denomination and therefore the criterion of free entry is violated. Labour unions were voluntary associations originally, but at the present time "closed shop" and "automatic check-off" requirements tend to give little freedom of entry and exit to many workers. Although *intensive* participation in either church or union is voluntary, it was decided to discuss these organizations separately. Tables presenting rate of participation exclude union and church membership unless otherwise specified.

During the interview, the respondents were given a list of organizations to aid them in recalling their membership. The respondents were asked the following question:

Could you tell me what clubs and organizations you belong to?
Do you belong to any like this?
  Labour Unions
  Social Clubs or Sports Clubs
  Parents/Teachers or Home and School Association
  Youth Groups (as a leader)
  Church Associated Groups
  Lodges
  Community Centres
  Organizations of people of the same nationality groups
  Political Associations
  Neighbourhood Improvement, Residents' or Ratepayers' Associations.

Of course the intensity of involvement in an organization is also an important consideration. A well-developed and frequently used instrument, the Chapin scale, was used to measure this area. For each organizational membership the respondent was asked the following series of questions:

Do you attend meetings?
Do you make a financial contribution to the organization?
Are you a member of any committee of that organization?
Do you hold any office in that organization (like President or Treasurer)?

On the basis of the replies to these questions each respondent could be assigned a score which reflects his overall participation in voluntary associations. The details of this procedure are more fully described by Delbert C. Miller (1964). On the basis of the Chapin Score, each respondents' extent of participation was classified as "none", "low" or "high". Those with no participation had scores of zero; those with low participation had scores of 1 - 8; those with high participation had scores greater than eight.

Finally, high, medium and low involvement in church and in labour union was defined. Degree of religious involvement was defined by frequency of church attendance and by acquaintance with the clergyman. Schematically, the various degrees of religious involvement are shown in Figure 1.

FIGURE 1. *Religious Involvement*

Frequency of Church Attendance

		HIGH	LOW
Acquaintance with Clergyman	HIGH	High religious involvement	Medium religious involvement
	LOW	Medium religious involvement	Low religious involvement

Similarly labour union involvement was measured by the combination of two dimensions. The first was extent of participation as indicated by attendance of union meetings and office holding. The second was the extent to which the respondent's membership was voluntary. The membership was considered voluntary if it was not a condition of employment or if the respondent felt he would join the union even if membership were not a condition of employment.

In the conclusion some consideration is given to social integration other than in the neighbourhood or formal organizations. This was measured by a 'non-neighbourhood integration' score derived from the sum of positive answers to questions concerning places visited and activities undertaken, outside the immediate neighbourhood.

All numerical data and items that could be appropriately scaled or reduced to 'dummy variables' were subjected to correlation analysis, using zero—order Pearson product—moment correlation coefficients and some partial correlations. A condensed version of the correlation matrix is included in Table 75, as a convenient means of summarising the findings, which will be presented in more detailed tabulations in the chapters that follow.

III

CHARACTERISTICS OF HOUSEHOLD HEADS
IN THE SURVEY AREAS

The population of the city of Toronto as a whole is notable for the high proportion who were born outside of Canada. In 1961 this was characteristic of 42 % of the City population and the proportion may have risen since. It was not surprising, therefore, to find that 62 % of the heads of household in the areas studied were foreign-born. The proportion of foreign-born was lower (39 %) in those areas currently under-going urban renewal or scheduled for development in the near future, compared with the remaining areas in which 65 % of the heads of household were foreign-born. In the sample as a whole, a large majority of the foreign-born were post-war immigrants, only 11 % having entered Canada in 1945 or earlier. It is important to note also that 51 % of the immigrants had been sponsored by a close relative when they entered Canada. Sponsors must provide the Federal Immigration authorities with guarantees of housing and financial support, or employment, for relatives entering the country. Sponsoring has given rise to chain migration, to the formation of close-knit networks of kith and kin in certain areas and to the phenomenon of "doubling"; that is, multiple households in single family dwellings.

A quarter of the foreign-born heads in the sample had entered Canada in 1966 or later and almost half since 1961. In other words, they are comparatively recent immigrants and represent an addition to the population since the censuses of 1961 and 1966 respectively. Fifty-five per cent of the foreign-born compared with 18 % of the native-born had lived in Metropolitan Toronto for eight years or less at the time of the survey. A third of the foreign-born compared with 56 % of the native-born respondents had lived in the neighbourhood (that is, within 5 blocks of their present residence) for nine years or more.

TABLE 4. *Length of Residence at Present Address by Birthplace*

Length of Residence	Native-born %	Foreign-born %	Total %
Two years and under	33	47	42
3-8 years	33	31	32
9 years and over	34	22	26
Total	100(n = 115)	100(n = 194)	100(N = 309)

$\chi^2 = 7.76$, 2 d.f. $p < .02 > .01$; Cramèr's V $= 0.16$

Table 4 shows that there were only marginally significant differences between native-born and foreign-born in length of residence at the present address. Although native-born respondents were more likely to have been resident at the present address three years or more, Table 4 indicates that there was considerable mobility even among the native-born households.

Ethnic Origins

Both the native-born and foreign-born populations were quite heterogeneous in terms of ethnic origins. In terms of the birthplace of the respondent's father forty-one per cent of the native-born heads were second generation immigrants, approximately 40 % of whom were not of British ethnic origin. Among the foreign-born, 16 % had English as the mother tongue. Many other languages were represented but the major concentrations were Italian (25 %), Portuguese (21 %) and Slavic (14 %). Taking the sample as a whole 55 % did not have English as the mother tongue.

At the time of the survey 42 % of the foreign-born were Canadian citizens. Of those who were not, a majority expected to become naturalized Canadian citizens in due course. When they first came to Canada, 10 % of the immigrants had planned to return to the former country eventually and a further 20 % were uncertain about their future plans. Of these the large majority now thought that it was more likely that they would settle permanently in Canada. When asked, "Do you feel now that you are fully a Canadian, or do you still feel as if you belong more in your old country?" 41 % of the immigrants felt now they belonged wholly in Canada. Seventeen per cent still felt they belonged wholly in the old country, and the remainder felt "part Canadian only." The partial acculturation of the immigrant heads was reflected in their use of radio and newspapers. Half the respondents read English-Canadian newspapers but 56 % read foreign-language newspapers. Furthermore, half the foreign-born respondents listened to radio programmes specially meant for listeners from their old country, 16 % doing so daily. Almost all those with a foreign mother tongue used this language at home but, more surprisingly, almost a quarter of the foreign-born used a language other than English at work.

Demographic and Socio-Economic Characteristics

Foreign-born heads of household tended to be younger than native-born heads, two-thirds of the former compared with 54 % of the latter being under 45 years. Although 84 % of all heads were male, 28 % of the native-born heads were female compared with only 10 % of the foreign-born. This was partly a reflection of the differences in family composition between native and foreign-born households. Table 5 shows that 10 % of all heads of house-

TABLE 5. *Family Type by Birthplace*

Family Type	Native-born %	Foreign-born %	Total %
Single person	12	9	10
Single person with extended kin and/or lodgers	0	1	0
Nuclear family	42	54	49
Childless family	19	14	16
Broken family	15	5	9
Nuclear family with extended kin and/or lodgers	7	11	10
Childless family with extended kin and/or lodgers	3	5	4
Broken family with extended kin and/or lodgers	2	2	2
Total	100(n = 120)	100(n = 196)	100(N = 316)

$\chi^2 = 13.45$,   7 d.f. $p < .06$;   Cramèr's $V = 0.21$

hold in the sample were single. There was no difference between native-born and foreign-born in this respect but native-born households were more likely to be childless. This probably reflects the age composition of the native-born heads and the fact that children would have grown up and left home. Native-born households were also significantly more likely to be broken homes through separation, divorce, or death of a spouse. This was characteristic of 15 % of the native-born households compared with 5 % of the foreign-born. Contrary to expectations there was no significant difference between native-born and foreign-born in the frequency with which households contained extended kin or lodgers. This was characteristic of 15 % of all households in the sample. This effectively disposes of the myth that immigrant families were frequently based upon an extended family or kinship system. It seems that the independent nuclear family is maintained despite the high proportion of households who share the same dwelling.

The occupational distribution of household heads is shown in Table 6. Approximately a quarter of the sample was engaged in managerial, professional and other white collar occupations. This was characteristic of a significantly higher proportion of native-born heads. Foreign-born heads were much more likely to be

TABLE 6.   *Occupation of Household Heads by Birthplace*

Occupation	Native-born %	Foreign-born %	Total %
Managerial occupations	6	6	6
Professional and			
Technical	8	8	8
Clerical and Sales	22	6	12
Service and Recreation	12	19	16
Transportation and			
Communication	11	4	7
Primary Occupations	3	1	2
Craftsmen, Production			
Process	20	32	27
Labourers	7	15	12
Occupation not stated,			
Refusal to answer	0	3	2
Not in Labour Force	11	6	8
Total	100(n = 120)	100(n = 196)	100(N = 316)

$\chi^2 = 34.41$,   7 d.f.   p < .001;   Cramèr's V = 0.35

employed as craftsmen, factory workers or labourers. In other words, there was a marked status differential between native and foreign-born heads using the conventional criterion of occupational prestige. This status differential was also reflected in the subjective class identification of the respondents, although to a lesser degree. Of the native-born heads 24 % described themselves as "middle class" compared with only 14 % of the foreign-born.

Differences in economic status were also evident although to a lesser degree when the distribution of family earnings were considered. The distribution of family income is shown in Table 7. It shows that about a third of the sample were earning less than $5,000 and slightly under one-third, $7,000 or more per annum at the time of the survey. When an adjustment was made for the number of earners per family, it was evident that the average income per earner was significantly less in the case of households of foreign-born heads.

TABLE 7. Family Income by Birthplace

Income	Native-born %	Foreign-born %	Total %
Under $1500	6	4	5
$1500-2999	10	5	7
$3000-3999	7	8	7
$4000-4999	8	15	13
$5000-5999	13	15	15
$6000-6999	12	11	11
$7000-7999	8	10	9
$8000-8999	7	6	6
$9000-9999	3	5	4
$10,000 or more	14	8	10
Don't Know / No Answer / Inapplicable	12	13	13
Total	100(n = 120)	100(n = 196)	100(N = 316)

$\chi^2 = 12.57$,   9 d.f.   p < .18;   Cramèr's V = 0.21

Housing Conditions and Satisfaction

Slightly under half the heads of household in the sample were owner-occupiers. However, there were significant differences between native-born and foreign-born respondents in this respect. Two-thirds of the former compared with only 45 % of the latter were renting accommodation. Of those who were renting, two-thirds expected to continue doing so for at least the next three years but, again, there was a greater propensity to purchase a house among the foreign-born. This is shown in Table 8. When asked, "If you could afford to do so, would you rather buy your own house right away or would you rather go on renting?" 68 % of all those renting said they would prefer to buy and there was no significant difference between native-born and foreign-born in this respect.

TABLE 8. *Plans to Buy or Continue Renting by Birthplace, Renters Only*

Plans to Buy/Rent	Native-born %	Foreign-born %	Total %
Go on Renting	77	59	68
Buy within three years	14	27	21
Don't Know/No Answer	9	14	11
Total	100(n = 78)	100(n = 88)	100(N = 166)

$\chi^2 = 6.136$, 2 d.f. $p < .05 > 0.2$; Cramèr's $V = 0.19$

It seems likely that the immigrant population saw home ownership as a more realistic possibility in the next three years because they thought in terms of buying property in the downtown area which might be sub-let for income purposes. In contrast the native-born population probably thought in terms of purchasing a house for single family occupation in a suburban or similar area.

Of the home owners, 6 % had not required a mortgage when first purchasing and this was more characteristic of the native-born heads. The latter were also more likely to have paid off original mortgages, two-thirds of those who had originally borrowed money for house purchase having done so among the native-born compared with only one-third of the foreign-born. A quarter of the native-born home owners compared with 13 % of the foreign-born also owned other property in addition to their own home. In purchasing the house two-thirds of the foreign-born had been assisted by a real estate salesman and in about half the cases the latter was of the same ethnic origin as the respondent. In only about one-third of the cases was the former owner of the house of the same ethnic group or nationality as the present owner, suggesting that there has been a substantial shift in the ethnic composition of these areas in recent years, at least as far as property ownership is concerned.

Of those renting accommodation, ninety per cent said that the landlord was a private person rather than a company. In the case of 40 % of the foreign-born and 16 % of the native-born, the landlord was a friend or relative of the tenant. Table 9 shows that in the case of 57 % of those renting, the ethnic origin of the

TABLE 9.   *Ethnicity of Landlord by Birthplace of Head of Household, Renters Only*

Ethnicity of Landlord	Native-born %	Foreign-born %	Total %
Same ethnicity as respondent	25	56	43
Different ethnicity from respondent	75	44	57
Total	100(n=59)	100(n=82)	100(N=141)
	$\chi^2=11.93$, 1 d.f. $p<.001$; Phi$=0.31$		

landlord was different from that of the tenant. In particular 75 % of the native-born tenants had landlords of a different origin suggesting that in these areas there was extensive property ownership by first and second generation immigrants who let accommodation for income purposes. Table 10 shows that native-born tenants were generally paying higher rents than foreign-born tenants in the areas studied but this could be related to the size and quality of the accommodation. Nevertheless, it is indicative of the important function which these areas serve in providing low rental accommodation for recently arrived immigrant families.

Respondents were asked "Have you heard of the Toronto Housing Registry where you can put your name down for public housing at low rentals?" Eigthy-three per cent of the native-born compared with only fifty per cent for the foreign-born had heard of the Registry and of those 25 % of the native-born and 17 % of the foreign-born had actually placed their names on the list. Of those who had not previously heard of the Toronto Housing Registry about half said that they would be interested in applying for low rental housing provided by the government. Forty-five per cent of all

TABLE 10. *Rent Paid by Birthplace, Renters Only*

Rent Paid	Native-born %	Foreign-born %	Total %
$26-50	10	9	10
$51-75	10	27	18
$76-100	26	33	30
$101-125	17	15	16
$126-150	23	3	12
$151-175	5	3	4
$176-200	1	2	2
Pay no rent	0	1	1
Don't Know/No Answer	8	7	7
Total	100(n=78)	100(n=88)	100(N=166)

$\chi^2 = 20.54$,   7 d.f. $p < .005$;   Cramèr's $V = 0.37$

renters positively approved of public housing and only 19 % expressed a definite disapproval. However, native-born respondents were more likely to disapprove or have mixed feelings about public housing than foreign-born. Respondents who were renting accommodation were asked "The Task Force on Housing recently recommended that the government help people with low incomes pay their rent instead of providing public housing. What do you think poorer families in this area would prefer?" Thirty-seven per cent said that they thought more public housing was desirable and 46 % considered help with rent would be preferable. There was no significant difference between native-born and foreign-born in this respect.

Housing Conditions

As the survey focussed upon those areas of the City of Toronto that were actually or potentially urban renewal areas it was not surprising to find that housing conditions were generally poor. Not all the houses in these areas were necessarily very old or dilapidated but there were a number of "pockets of poor housing" which, in due course, will be due for complete demolition. As the 1966 survey by the Metropolitan Toronto Planning Board showed, many of the older houses were structurally sound and would simply need rehabilitation and improved maintenance. However, compared with the high quality of housing and standard of amenity in the rest of Metropolitan Toronto the inhabitants of these areas were undoubtedly living in comparatively poor housing conditions. It was evident also that the foreign-born households were substantially worse off than the native-born. Including kitchens, bedrooms, living rooms, and finished rooms in attic or basement but excluding bathrooms, halls, vestibules and rooms used purely for business purposes, the average number of rooms available to native-born households was 5.5 compared with 5 for the foreign-born households. However, this must be considered in relation to the size of the households in question. Foreign-born households were likely to be considerably larger than native-born households. In fact, the average number of persons per native-born household was 3.5 compared with 5 persons per foreign-born household. This meant that many foreign-born households were quite over-crowded. The average number of persons per room in native-born households was .6 compared with 1 person per room on average in foreign-born households.

Another factor affecting the quality of housing was the extent of "doubling". The survey found that there was more than one household at 46 % of the selected addresses. However, 72 % of the native-born households were the only household at that address compared with 41 % of the foreign born. This is shown in Table 11.

TABLE 11. *Number of Households at Address by Birthplace*

Number of Households	Native-born %	Foreign-born %	Total %
One	72	41	54
Two	15	39	31
Three	3	10	8
Four	6	5	5
Five	3	2	2
Six	0	1	0
Seven	0	1	0
Eight	1	0	0
Don't Know/No Answer	0	1	0
Total	100(n=120)	100(n=196)	100(N=316)

$\chi^2 = 34.61$, 7 d.f. $p < .001$;   Cramèr's $V = 0.33$

A household in this case was defined in terms of those people who shared the same eating facilities. It was comparatively rare for more than one family to share such facilities. In fact, in only three per cent of the sampled households was there more than one family unit. However, the fact that almost half the sampled households were in shared dwellings meant that the facilities of the dwelling were often shared by several families. For example 23 % of native-born families and 31 % of foreign-born were sharing the use of a bathroom. It is evident that the major housing problems of the areas studied are those arising from the multiple-occupation of single family dwellings with consequent overcrowding and shared use of facilities.

Despite these problems overall satisfaction with present housing conditions was remarkably high. In interpreting the evidence it must be kept in mind that in assessing satisfaction the respondents were probably taking into acount the low cost of the housing and the convenience of the locality. Table 12 shows that a third of the heads of household in the sample said that they were very satisfied

TABLE 12. *Satisfaction with Accommodation by Birthplace*

Satisfaction	Native-born %	Foreign-born %	Total %
Very Satisfied	32	35	34
Satisfied	43	42	42
In between	13	19	17
Not Satisfied*	12	4	7
Total	100(n = 119)	100(n = 192)	100(N = 311)

* Includes : "Dissatisfied," $\chi^2 = 8.82$,   3 d.f. $p < .05 > 0.2$;
         "Very Dissatisfied"   Cramèr's $V = 0.17$

with the house in which they were living. Less than a quarter did not express any degree of satisfaction and there appeared to be no significant difference between native-born and foreign-born in their feelings about present accomodation.

Conclusion

It is evident that there were important differences between immigrant and Canadian-born householders in economic status and housing. Although the foreign-born were in lower status occupations and earned less they maintained family incomes close to average through contributions of other members of the household. Immigrants were more likely to be home owners but they were also more likely to be in multiple occupation of dwellings, which were often let for income purposes.

It remains to consider what influence these differences had upon integration into the neighbourhood and, in turn, the effect of this upon attitudes to urban renewal.

IV

NEIGHBOURHOOD SATISFACTION AND INTEGRATION

Although there was relative homogeneity with regard to housing satisfaction there was greater variation with regard to neighbourhood satisfaction. Table 13 shows that there was a slight difference statistically non-significant, between native-born and foreign-born,

TABLE 13. *Neighbourhood Satisfaction by Birthplace*

Neighbourhood Satisfaction	Native-born %	Foreign-born %	Total %
Very Satisfied	22	36	31
Satisfied	43	39	40
Not Satisfied*	35	25	29
Total	100(n = 113)	100(n = 189)	100(N = 302)

* Includes: "In between," "Dissatisfied," $\chi^2 = 7.33$ 2 d.f. $p < .05 > .02$;
        "Very Dissatisfied"   Cramèr's $V = 0.16$

the latter generally having a higher satisfaction with neighbourhood in which they were living than the native-born. Given that the sample consisted of actual-potential urban renewal areas it is important to note the very small proportion of the household heads (7 %) who actually expressed dissatisfaction with the neighbourhood. However, when specifically asked to indicate anything which they disliked about the neighbourhood the large majority of respondents were able to name some characteristic. The physical characteristics of the neighbourhood were mentioned most often followed by social characteristics. Table 14, appearing below, shows that foreign-born respondents were most likely to mention

TABLE 14. *Reasons for Dissatisfaction with Neighbourhood by Birthplace*

Reasons for Dissatisfaction	Native-born %	Foreign-born %	Total %
Economic-housing	0	0	0
Accessibility-convenience of facilities	4	4	4
Neighbourhood-physical qualities	38	53	46
Neighbourhood-social qualities	32	12	21
Family and Friends in neighbourhood	5	4	4
Ethnic reasons	8	9	9
Other	7	6	7
Dislike everything	4	3	3
Don't know/No Answer/ Inapplicable	2	9	6
Total	100(n=85)	100(n=98)	100(N=183)

$\chi^2 = 10.3$, 6 d.f. $p < .10$; Cramèr's $V = 0.24$

that they disliked the physical characteristics of the neighbourhood whereas the native-born were almost equally divided between those who mentioned physical qualities and social qualities. Only 9 % of those expressing any dislikes mentioned the ethnic composition of the area as a factor which they disliked but the relatively low social status of the area was viewed negatively, particularly by the native-born.

There was greater unanimity among native-born and foreign-born concerning the factors which they liked most about the neighbourhood, although foreign-born were again more likely to approve of the social qualities including the proximity of family, friends and others of the same ethnic group. The factor mentioned most often was the accessibility of the neighbourhood and its convenience for a variety of purposes. Eight out of ten of those in employment found it easy or very easy to get to work each day. Forty-two per cent of those working took less than twenty minutes to get to work and only 15 % took more than forty-five minutes. Sixteen per cent walked, thirty-eight used T.T.C. and forty-three per cent an automobile to get to work. Nine out of ten of the respondents considered the neighbourhood convenient for family shopping and almost two-thirds emphasized that it was very convenient. There was no difference between native-born and foreign-born in this respect but there was a significant difference in the shopping habits of the two groups. Table 15 indicates that the native-born families

TABLE 15. *"Shopping Habits" by Birthplace*

Shopping Habits	Native-born %	Foreign-born %	Total %
Large chain stores, supermarkets	73	42	53
Ethnic stores and supermarkets	6	44	30
Other	13	8	10
Don't know/No Answer/ Inapplicable	8	6	7
Total	100(n = 120)	100(n = 196)	100(N = 316)

$\chi^2 = 52.54$,   2 d.f. $p < .001$;   Cramèr's $V = 0.42$

were far more likely to use large chain stores and supermarkets whereas the foreign-born population more often patronized ethnic stores and smaller supermarkets. Two-thirds of all respondents emphasized that the store at which they did most of their shopping was within walking distance. Although the Kensington Market is an important amenity for those living in the immediate vicinity it was used by only a third of the respondents in this sample. One in five of the foreign-born population compared with only 4 % in the native-born said that they shopped at the Kensington Market weekly or more often. Those living at a distance from the Kensington Market were more likely to use other local ethnic stores. The latter were patronized by 20 % of the native-born compared with 56 % of the foreign-born respondents. The small stores and markets, particularly of the ethnic type, were clearly serving an important function for many of the residents of the areas studied.

The majority of families in the sample with children said that their children were going to a local school that was also conveniently close at hand. Of those children 60 % of the foreign-born household heads and 44 % of the native-born said that they were very satisfied with the quality of the schooling the children were getting.

Neighbourhood Integration

In order to ascertain whether the heads of household in the areas studied identified with the neighbourhood in which they were living they were asked "Do you feel at home in this neighbourhood: that is, is it the place in Canada where you feel you belong?" Seventy-three per cent gave an affirmative answer to this question and there was no difference in this respect between native-born and foreign-born. Those who gave a negative answer were asked "Where in Canada would you call home?" Twenty-three per cent indicated a place elsewhere in Metropolitan Toronto, 11 % elsewhere in Ontario, 10 % elsewhere in Canada and 25 % said "nowhere in Canada."

Most people correctly perceived the neighbourhood in which they were living as quite heterogeneous from an income and an ethnic point of view. However, 21 % of the foreign-born compared with 8 % of the native-born thought that most people living in that neighbourhood were of the same ethnic group as the respondent. Twenty-three percent of the native-born compared with 10 % of the foreign-born felt that their neighbourhood consisted mainly of one ethnic group different from that of the respondent. Approximately a third of both the native and foreign-born respondents expressed a preference for living in a neighbourhood where most people were the same ethnic group as themselves. A preference for living near others of the same language and cultural way of life was the reason most often given for this choice.

More than a third of the household heads had relatives or in-laws living in the same neighbourhood. Although the foreign-born were slightly more likely to have relatives in the neigbourhood the difference was not statistically significant. However, it must be remembered that the average length of residence of the foreign-born was much shorter than that of the native-born respondents. When asked, "If you had a choice, would you prefer to live close to relatives?" it was evident that this was a situation much more often preferred by the foreign-born than the native-born heads of household. Table 16 shows the distribution of answers to this question. It indicates that, while two-thirds of the native-born were opposed to living close to relatives only one-third of the foreign-born were negative. When asked reasons for their preference the foreign-born more often gave both practical utilitarian reasons and positive affective reasons for wishing to live near relatives while the native-born emphasized a variety of negative aspects of living close to relatives. Although neither the native-born nor foreign-born respondents were wholly dependent upon people living in the neighbourhood for their social contacts, one-third of the latter compared with a quarter of the former said that most of the people

TABLE 16. *Preference for Living Close to Relatives by Birthplace*

Preferred Closeness to Relatives	Native-born %	Foreign-born %	Total %
Would prefer to live close to relatives	18	49	37
Would prefer *not* to live close to relatives	67	36	48
It depends	15	15	15
Total	100(n=117)	100(n=181)	100(N=298)

$\chi^2 = 33.5$,   2 d.f. $p < .0005$;   Cramèr's $V = 0.34$

they knew well were living in their own neighbourhood. The combined effects of social networks based upon kith and kin that were focused upon the neighbourhood meant that the foreign-born were more likely to exhibit a strong attachment to the neighbourhood and resist the idea of moving from it.

This view was confirmed by the "neighbourhood integration score" to which reference was made in the section on survey methodology. Correlation analysis indicated that five items were closely associated with each other and could be used as a basis of a measure of neighbourhood integration. The items were: Satisfaction with the neighbourhood; Feeling at home in the neighbourhood; Satisfaction with present house; Ownership of house; Having relatives living in the neighbourhood. These items were also positively but less strongly correlated with length of residence in the neighbourhood, convenience of work and shopping as well as stating that most people known well lived in the neighbourhood.

The neighbourhood integration score, on a scale from 0 to 6, is shown in Table 17. The mean score was 2.8 with a standard deviation of 1.6.

TABLE 17. *Neighbourhood Integration Score by Birthplace*

Neighbourhood Integration	Native-born %	Foreign-born %	Total %
0 (Low)	9	7	8
1	20	13	15
2	27	17	20
3	9	25	22
4	22	17	18
5	10	15	12
6 (High)	3	6	5
Total	100(n=120)	100(n=196)	100(N=316)

$\chi^2 = 12.68$, 6 d.f. $p < .05$; Cramèr's $V = 0.20$

Despite the association with length of residence in the neighbourhood and the fact that the native-born had a longer period of residence on average than the foreign-born, the latter tended to score higher on the neighbourhood integration score. Of the native-born 56 % score below the median compared with 37 % of the foreign-born heads.

The validity of the neighbourhood integration score as a measure of attachment to the area was indicated by its close association with the intention to remain in the neighbourhood or to move elsewhere. This is shown in Table 18. As the neighbourhood integration score increased so the proportion of the respondents who indicated an intention to move declined. For example, 83 % of those with a neighbourhood integration score of zero planned to move, compared with only 6 % of those with the highest score. This relationship held good even after nativity and length of residence in the neighbourhood were controlled. When only those who expected to move were considered the neighbourhood integration score was correlated with the imminence of the intended move. Those with below average scores were more likely to be expecting to move immediately or within one year than those with average or higher scores. In the case of the foreign-born those with average or higher neighbourhood integration scores who planned to move were more likely to say that they intended to move to another dwelling in the same neighbourhood.

It was originally expected that there would be an association between the neighbourhood integration score and various measures

TABLE 18. *Percent with Plans to Move by Length of Residence and Neighbourhood Integration Score Controlling for Birthplace*

Neigh-bourhood Integration Score	Native-born				Foreign-born				Total	
	Resident in Neighbourhood				Resident in Neighbourhood					
	Under 9 years		9 years and over		Under 9 years		9 years and over			
	%	n/N	%	n/N	%	n/N	%	n/N	%	n/N
0	100	7/7	75	3/4	81	9/11	50	1/2	83	20/24
1	67	8/12	78	7/9	52	11/21	50	3/6	60	29/48
2	63	7/11	53	9/17	38	9/24	50	4/8	47	29/60
3	40	2/5	21	3/14	35	12/34	50	7/14	33	24/67
4	37	3/8	13	2/15	32	7/22	40	4/10	29	16/55
5	20	1/5	0	0/5	25	3/12	12	2/16	15	6/38
6	0	0/0	0	0/3	11	1/9	0	0/6	6	1/18
Total	58	28/48	36	24/67	39	52/133	34	21/62	41	125/310

of socio-economic status. It is generally assumed that a close attachment to a particular neighbourhood is more characteristic of the manual working class and lower income groups than of other social classes. However, within the neighbourhoods studied in this survey there appeared to be no association between the neighbourhood integration score and various measures of status, including income, occupation and subjective class identification. This lack of association persisted after the introduction of controls for nativity and length of residence in the neighbourhood. Nevertheless, for the foreign-born only, there was a highly significant and negative association between years of education and neighbourhood integration. In fact, low education largely explained the higher integration level of the foreign-born, as the association of nativity with integration ceased to be significant when education was taken into account. Age also proved to be positively correlated with neighbourhood integration for the foreign but not the native-born.

Length of Residence and Mobility

A question of particular interest is the function which the neighbourhoods may perform for the immigrants and ethnic groups. Specifically, are these neighbourhoods "zones-of-transition," areas in which the immigrant settles temporarily, only until he is more able, for financial or other reasons, to move to another area; or would it be more accurate to characterize these neighbourhoods as relatively stable residential neighbourhoods? In answering this question, two types of data will be considered; namely, data relating to actual length of residence and data dealing with plans to move. Thus, both actual mobility and potential mobility, or motility, will be considered.

The actual lengths of residence at the present address have already been shown in Table 4 above. As may be seen from these figures, the native-born population has a longer average length of residence than the foreign-born, with median length of residence for the native-born population being about 6 years, as opposed to 3.5 for the foreign-born.

It is instructive, at this point to compare the figures for these neighbourhoods to those for the remainder of Toronto. While a detailed breakdown is not available, figures obtained from the Metropolitan Planning Board of Toronto indicate that thirty per cent of the population have resided at their present address for more than 10 years, and seventeen per cent of the population have resided at their present address for less than 1 year. Thus, it appears likely that the native-born segment of the sample exhibits residential patterns highly representative of the remainder of the total Toronto population.

While the native-born population in our sample has a longer average length of residence than the foreign-born population, other characteristics of the population must be examined before greater stability can be attributed to the native-born. Age differences between the two subsamples are important: forty-three per cent of the native-born population was forty-five years old or older, as opposed to only thirty-two per cent of the foreign-born population. This, of course, is in accordance with the general finding that the highest rates of migration occur among young people. (Bogue, 1959) The more important implication of the greater age of the native-born for our study is that this group simply has had greater opportunity for residential stability. Table 19 presents the data for length of residence in Toronto for our sample.

The native-born population, as expected, has a much greater average length of residence in Toronto than the foreign-born

TABLE 19. *Length of Residence in Toronto by Birthplace*

Length of Residence	Native-born %	Foreign-born %	Total %
0-2 years	6	19	15
3-8 years	11	35	25
9 years and over	83	46	60
Total	100(n = 117)	100(n = 196)	100(N = 313)

$\chi^2 = 40.71$, 2 d.f. $p < .001$; Cramèr's $V = 0.36$

population. The proposition that the foreign-born population is less stable residentially than the native-born population must be examined more closely in light of this fact. To do this, two sub-samples have been compared on median length of residence at present address as opposed to length of residence in Toronto, and, as well have computed weighted averages for each type of length of residence. The median lengths of residence at present address for the two sub-samples are 6 and 3.5 years respectively; for length of residence in Toronto, the figures are 11.4 and 7.8 years. Based on these figures, the differences in residential stability are reduced. Another method of comparing the two populations is to compute a weighted average, or mean number of years in residence both in Toronto, and at the present address. Using this measure, the results are as follows; length of residence in Toronto, 14 years for native-born, 8.9 years for foreign-born; length of residence at present address, 7.2 years for native-born, 5.4 years for foreign-born. It appears that there is no substantial difference in the residential stability of the native-born as opposed to the foreign-born, if the shorter length of residence in Toronto of the latter group is taken into account.

Finally, potential mobility or motility is also relevant to an assessment of residential stability. As previously mentioned, the indicator which we shall utilize here is the question of plans to move by our respondents. Obviously this represents an imperfect indicator to the extent that people's behaviour deviates from their plans and expectations, but it is at present the best measure available.

Table 20 presents the stated plans to move of the native-born compared to the foreign-born.

Slightly fewer of the foreign-born than of the native-born respondents have plans to move from the present dwelling. However, given the fact that an individual with only the vaguest plans to move would probably have answered this question with a "yes", it seems safe to regard these figures as indicating fairly low levels of motility

TABLE 20. *Plans to Move from Present Dwelling by Birthplace*

Plans to Move	Native-born %	Foreign-born %	Total %
Do have plans to move	46	40	42
Do *not* have plans to move	54	60	58
Total	100(n=115)	100(n=185)	100(N=300)

$\chi^2=1.40$, N.S.

in both populations. This interpretation is supported by the responses to the question "How definite are your plans to move and how soon do you expect to move?" presented below in Table 21.

TABLE 21. *Immediacy of Plans to Move by Birthplace*
Potential Movers Only

Plans to Move	Native-born %	Foreign-born %	Total %
Final plans to move made	20	15	18
Expects to move within one year	12	19	16
Expects to move within five years	16	14	14
Expects to move eventually, or depends on circum-stances	52	52	52
Total	100(n=56)	100(n=78)	100(N=134)

$\chi^2=1.32$, N.S.

Finally, it is interesting to note the pattern which emerges from a cross-tabulation of plans to move by length of residence at present address. Table 22 shows interesting trends although the differences between native and foreign-born are not large enough to be significant. In particular, while plans to move are strongly related to length of residence for the native-born population, with those individuals with the shortest length of residence expressing plans to move most often, this pattern does not hold for the foreign-born population, where there is a curvilinear relationship with length of residence. Also interesting is the fact that a higher proportion of long-term foreign-born residents than native-born residents expressed plans to move.

TABLE 22.   *Percentage of Potential Movers by Length of Residence and Birthplace*

Length of Residence	Native-born		Foreign-born	
	%	n/N	%	n/N
0-2 years	66	25/38	41	38/92
3-8 years	47	15/38	30	18/60
9 years and over	21	8/39	38	16/42
Percent Potential Movers	44	51/115	37	72/194

Conclusion

Little evidence has been found in our sample which supports the view that the urban renewal areas, which are by and large characterized by concentration of immigrants and ethnic groups, are serving as zones-of-transition. Rather, our data indicate that these areas have patterns of residential stability comparable to the remainder of Toronto. Patterns of residential stability appear to be similar for the foreign-born and the native-born populations, with the latter in fact slightly more motile than the former, except for long-term residents. There is a low level of plans to move from the neighbourhood for both sub-samples, and few respondents stated any definite plans to move in the near future. Neighbourhood satisfaction among our respondents was quite high, with sixty-one per cent of the native-born population, and seventy-two per cent of the foreign-born population expressing satisfaction with the neighbourhood as a whole.

In the light of the levels of neighbourhood integration and satisfaction exhibited by the respondents it is important to consider what their attitudes would be toward policies intended to improve these areas by rehabilitation, on the one hand, or expropriation and clearance on the other.

V

ATTITUDES TOWARDS URBAN RENEWAL

Questions in the survey concerning urban renewal were prefaced by a statement made by the interviewer as follows, "Now I have some questions on your opinions about housing and urban renewal. By urban renewal I mean local government action to improve parts of Toronto by fixing up old houses or by rebuilding." In interpreting the results of the study the possibility must be kept in mind that these remarks predisposed the respondent to a fairly favourable attitude towards urban renewal as an activity designed "to improve parts of Toronto." It is possible that if the interviewers had been instructed to offer a rather different description of the nature and purpose of urban renewal the responses would have been different.

Householders living in the areas studied who had been rehoused in public housing as a result of urban renewal were deliberately excluded from the sample. Therefore it is likely that comparatively few of the respondents had personal experience of the effects of urban renewal. However, 15 % indicated that they had friends or neighbours who had been affected or expected shortly to be affected by urban renewal. A little under a quarter of the sample were aware of government plans to improve their neighbourhood or to tear down houses for redevelopment. As would be expected, the proportion who were aware of urban renewal plans was considerably higher (48 %) in the two sub-strata which covered neighbourhoods for which there were imminent plans compared with respondents in the remaining areas studied, of whom only 19 % were aware of any government plans. Almost half the respondents felt that City Hall did not keep local residents sufficiently informed of the plans for their area and this view was most marked in the case of native-born respondents.

When represented in the way described by the interviewer the large majority of heads of households were favourable towards the idea of urban renewal in their own neighbourhood. This is shown in Table 23. Although native-born respondents were slightly more

TABLE 23. *Attitude toward Urban Renewal in Neighbourhood by Birthplace*

Urban Renewal	Native-born %	Foreign-born %	Total %
Very much in favour	46	40	43
Mildly in favour	23	15	18
Don't care	14	16	15
Mildly opposed	5	7	6
Very much opposed	5	7	6
Don't Know/No Answer/ Inapplicable	7	15	12
Total	100(n = 120)	100(n = 196)	100(N = 316)
	$\chi^2 = 3.86$, N.S.		

inclined to express favourable attitudes toward urban renewal the difference between them and the foreign-born respondents was not significant statistically.

Respondents were not specifically asked to distinguish between rehabilitation of property and its clearance for development purposes. However, they were asked to indicate whether they considered it was "all right to force people to sell their homes or to force people to move out of their homes in order to build a school." The same question was asked concerning a freeway or bridge and concerning new apartments. As would be expected the proportion indicating approval of clearance for these purposes was much lower than the proportion expressing approval of urban renewal in general. Table 24 shows the percentage expressing outright disapproval of each type of forced move and distinguishes between native-born and foreign-born. The remaining respondents were divided fairly evenly between those who approved clearance for these purposes and those who gave a conditional reply. It is evident that opposition was greatest towards clearance for building new apartments and least in the case of a new school. Some of the neighbourhoods studied would be affected if the Allen (Spadina) Expressway or Highway 400 were extended.

TABLE 24. *Percent Disapproving of Forced Move by Birthplace*

Reason for Move	Native-born %	Foreign-born %	Total %	Signif-icance
Forced move to build a school	53	36	44	*
Forced move to build a freeway or a bridge	56	43	48	N.S.
Forced move to build new apartments	62	54	57	N.S.
Base for % (N)	(120)	(196)	(316)	

$*\chi^2=9.06$, 1 d.f. $p<.003$; phi $= 0.18$

Therefore the reply to the question on forcing people to move in order to build a freeway or a bridge is of particular interest. Almost half the household heads gave an outright "No" in answer to this question and only 28 % expressed approval. In the case of all items there was a tendency for native-born to express stronger disapproval than foreign-born respondents. In the event of a home owner being forced to move, two-thirds of all respondents consider that he should receive the replacement cost of his dwelling rather than the market or salable value.

The attitudes toward urban renewal described so far have been of a somewhat abstract type. In order to ascertain more exactly the way in which the respondents themselves would feel if they were directly affected they were asked "If you had to move because of urban renewal, how would you feel about it?" They were given five previously defined responses from which they could choose. The distribution of their answers is set out in Table 24. A quarter of the respondents indicated that they would definitely resent being moved and a further 11 % indicated that they might miss the place in which they were living. There was no significant difference between native-born and foreign-born heads of household in this respect.

It may be surprising to note that almost two-thirds of the sample were fairly positive about urban renewal in general. In interpreting this finding it may be necessary to keep in mind that the respondents may have gained the impression from the interview that appropriate compensation and/or alternative accommodation would probably be made available to them in such a contingency. Although this

TABLE 25. *Attitude to Forced Relocation for Urban Renewal by Birthplace*

Forced Relocation	Native-born %	Foreign-born %	Total %
Would definitely like to get out of here	7	6	6
Wouldn't mind trying a different place to live	41	36	38
Don't care	12	14	13
Might miss living here	7	13	11
Would definitely resent being moved	27	25	26
Don't Know/No Answer/ Inapplicable	6	6	6
Total	100(n = 120)	100(n = 196)	100(N = 316)

$$\chi^2 = 3.99, \text{N.S.}$$

was never stated by the interviewers it is an inference that may have been drawn from the previous questions.

The preceding discussion is summarized by Table 26, which presents the proportion of native-born and foreign-born approving of urban renewal and forced relocation for various purposes.

TABLE 26. *Proportion in Favour of Urban Renewal and Forced Relocation by Birthplace*

Renewal and relocation	Native-born %	Foreign-born %	Total %	Phi
Urban renewal in general	69	56	61	0.13 $p < .02$
Respondent's own relocation for urban renewal *	48	43	44	N.S.
Forced relocation for school	18	40	31	0.23 $p < .001$
Forced relocation for freeway	18	33	27	0.16 $p < .01$
Forced relocation for apartments	13	27	22	0.16 $p < .01$
Base for % (N)	(120)	(196)	(316)	

* This is the only item directly involving the R's own relocation. The other items were phrased in more general terms, implying anyone's relocation.

At least two significant patterns emerge from these responses. First, while both the native-born and the foreign-born populations responded generally positively to the general concept of urban renewal, as seen by the response to question one, this positive response diminished greatly when the respondents were asked to state their attitudes toward the prospect of being forced to relocate. Second, this reduction of positive responses was much more prominent in the native-born population than in the foreign-born population; thus while the native-born respondents were more positive when asked about urban renewal in general, or how they would feel if forced to move because of urban renewal, they were more negative when asked about their feeling if forced to move for other, more specific reasons. For example, while sixty-nine per cent of the native-born respondents were generally in favour of urban renewal, only 13 per cent responded positively when asked how they would feel if they were forced to move in order to build new apartments.

Factors Influencing Attitudes Toward Urban Renewal

The variables other than ethnicity which may be expected to influence attitudes toward urban renewal fall into three categories: social class, life cycle stage and social integration particularly in the neighbourhood.

It was expected that middle-class respondents would be more favourable to urban renewal and forced relocation than working-class respondents. Presumably, better-educated, higher-income respondents would have a greater desire for changes in their residential area which would bring it close to middle-class norms regarding housing standards. In addition, middle-class people would have better resources for finding a new residence if they were forced to relocate because of urban renewal or development.

Surprisingly, income and education have very little effect on attitudes toward urban renewal. When occupational status is used as the indicator of social class, however, the expectations were supported for the foreign-born population, as demonstrated in Table 27.

Among the native-born, there is no significant difference in attitude toward relocation because of urban renewal among white

TABLE 27. *Occupational Status by Attitude toward Forced Relocation for Urban Renewal, Controlling for Birthplace*

Occupational Status	Native-born				Foreign-born			
	In favour %	"It depends" %	Opposed %	N	In favour %	"It depends" %	Opposed %	N
White Collar	59	10	31	(42)	75	19	6	(36)
Blue Collar	48	15	37	(59)	38	13	49	(141)
Total	52	13	35	(101)	45	14	41	(177)
$\chi^2 = 1.59$, N.S.				$\chi^2 = 22.95$, 2 d.f.	$p < .001$;		Cramèr's $V = 0.36$	

and blue collar workers, although the result is in the expected direction. About half of each group was in favour, one-third was opposed and the remainder were uncertain. Among the foreign-born, however, distinct differences in attitude appeared. Three quarters of the white collar workers would not object to moving because of urban renewal, with more than a third of the blue-collar foreign-born feeling this way. The interesting thing is that half of the blue-collar foreign-born tend to register disapproval of forced relocation, suggesting a stronger attachment to the area than other groups.

The attitude of this group is rather uncertain until they are actually confronted with concrete instances of forced relocation.

The respondent's perception of his own social class was not significantly related to the various attitudes about urban renewal. There was a slight tendency for foreign-born individuals who did perceive themselves as being definitely in a given social class to be more negative toward forced relocation because of urban renewal.

Age proved to be the single most important predictor of opposition to urban renewal and, particularly, to the respondent's own forced relocation as a result of clearance for any purpose. The relationship for the sample as a whole is shown in Table 28. There was a slightly greater association between age and opposition in the case of the native-born, but the correlation persisted even after the effects of ethnicity, length of residence and other variables were partialled out. It is understandable that the disruptions likely to follow from renewal, even the rehabilitation of a neighbourhood,

TABLE 28. *Opposition to Own Forced Move by Age*

| | Age | | | | |
	34 years and under %	35-44 years %	45-64 years %	65 years and over %	Total %
Not opposed	72	59	62	28	61
Opposed*	28	41	38	72	39
Total	100 n=72	100 n=96	100 n=102	100 n=25	100 N=295

$\chi^2=15.33$,   3 d.f. $p<.002$;   Cramèr's $V=0.23$

* Includes those stating "I might miss this place" and "I would definitely resent being moved."

are likely to be most threatening to its older inhabitants. Younger people, as well as being less conservative, have greater opportunities for mobility and re-establishment elsewhere.

Supposedly, the more integrated a person is in the neighbourhood, the more he would approve of those aspects of urban beneficial to it and the more he would oppose forced relocation for purposes such as schools, freeways and apartment buildings. The answers to the questions about urban renewal in *general* and about forced relocation for schools, freeways or apartments in *general* did not vary with degree of neighbourhood integration. This suggests that the answers given to questions concerning the propriety of such

TABLE 29. *Percent who would oppose Forced Relocation for Urban Renewal by Length of Residence and Neighbourhood Integration, Controlling for Birthplace*

Neigh-bourhood Integration Score	Native-born				Foreign-born				Total	
	Resident in Neighbourhood				Resident in Neighbourhood					
	Under 9 years		9 years and over		Under 9 years		9 years and over			
	%	n/N	%	n/N	%	n/N	%	n/N	%	n/N
Low	27	8/30	23	7/30	21	12/56	6	1/16	21	28/132
Average and high	28	5/18	51	19/37	49	38/77	54	25/46	49	87/178
Total	27	13/48	39	26/67	38	50/133	27	26/62	37	115/310

action were based on general principles or diffuse feelings, rather than on the individual's identification with his own locality.

However the results for the respondent's *own* forced relocation for urban renewal *were* influenced by the neighbourhood integration score. This is shown in Table 29.

It is evident that the proportion who would resent being moved was much higher in the case of those with high integration scores, except in the case of the native-born who had lived in the area for less than nine years.

Table 30 supports the argument that motility as indicated by plans to move varies inversely with neighbourhood satisfaction.

TABLE 30. *Satisfaction with Neighbourhood by Plans to Move Controlling for Birthplace*

Plans to Move	Native-born			Foreign-born		
	Satisfied with neighbour- hood	Dissatisfied with neighbour- hood	N	Satisfied with neighbour- hood	Dissatisfied with neighbour- hood	N
Plans to move %	44	56	(48)	56	44	(71)
No plans to move %	80	20	(60)	86	14	(108)
Total	64	36	(108)	74	26	(179)

$\chi^2 = 15.2$, 1 d.f. $p < .001$, Phi $= 0.37$ $\chi^2 = 19.9$, 1 d.f. $p < .001$, Phi $= 0.29$

Since plans to move are inversely related to neighbourhood satisfaction, a component of neigbourhood integration which in turn varies inversely with approval for the respondent's own relocation for urban renewal, a positive relationship between plans to move and approval for urban renewal was expected.

Generally plans to move were found to be strongly related to the attitudes expressed by the foreign-born group with less effect in the native-born group. However, the particular attitudes toward *forced relocation* because of urban renewal were related in similar fashion to plans to move for native-born and foreign-born; therefore, the results in Table 31 are for the whole sample.

About two-thirds of those who had plans to move had no objection to their own forced relocation for urban renewal. On the other

TABLE 31. *Attitude toward Forced Relocation by Plans to Move because of Urban Renewal*

Plans to Move	Satisfied with Relocation for Urban Renewal	"It depends"	Opposed to Relocation for Urban Renewal	Total
Plans to move %	67	14	19	100 (n = 119)
No plans to move %	34	13	53	100 (n = 166)
Total	47	14	39	100(N = 285)

$$\chi^2 = 35.8, \ 2 \ \text{d.f.} \quad p < .001; \quad \text{Cramèrs} \ V = 0.34$$

hand only a third of those who had no plans to move agreed with the majority of potential movers. The non-movers, however, expressed a much higher level of opposition to forced relocation because of urban renewal.

Other significant differences in attitudes related to urban renewal and potential mobility appeared only for foreign-born, although the results were in the same direction for native-born. Table 32 shows that those who plan to move are more likely to approve generally of urban renewal in their part of Toronto.

TABLE 32. *Attitude toward Urban Renewal by Plans to Move, Foreign-born Only*

Plans to Move	In Favour of Urban Renewal	Opposed to Urban Renewal	Total
Plans to move %	76	24	100 (n = 66)
No plans to move %	56	44	100 (n = 93)
Total	64	36	100(N = 159)

$$\chi^2 = 6.61, \ 1 \ \text{d.f.} \quad p < .02 > .01; \quad \text{Phi} = 0.20$$

Three-quarters of those who plan to move favour urban renewal in general, while only a little more than half of those who don't plan to move are in favour.

Opposition to forced relocation for a freeway is much stronger among those foreign-born who don't plan to move. Those who do plan to move are not much more likely to be in favour of forced relocation for a freeway; rather they are more likely to be uncertain, as indicated in Table 33.

TABLE 33. *Attitude toward Forced Relocation for Freeway or Bridge by Plans to Move, Foreign-born Only*

Plans to move	In Favour of Forced Relocation for a Freeway or Bridge	"It depends"	Opposed to Forced Relocation for a Freeway or Bridge	Total
Plans to move %	37	31	32	100 (n=74)
No plans to move %	31	17	52	100 (n=111)
Total	33	23	44	100(N=185)

$$\chi^2 = 8.21, \ 2 \ \text{d.f.} \quad p < .02 > .01; \quad \text{Cramèrs} \ V = 0.21$$

Generally the relationship between plans to move and approval for urban renewal is not surprising. Those who plan to move are less attached to the neighbourhood and less satisfied with it. Probably they are more aware of and sensitive to those problems of the area which need some form of urban renewal as a solution. In addition, the idea of forced relocation is not as objectionable to those who plan to move in any case.

Another variable which can be expected to influence attitudes toward urban renewal is satisfaction with housing. Presumably those who are satisfied with their present dwelling would be more opposed to urban renewal than those who are dissatisfied. Again, much more variation was found within the foreign-born population than within the native-born population. Generally, a high degree of satisfaction with one's dwelling varies directly with uncertainty toward the idea of urban renewal and forced relocation, as Table 34 demonstrates for the foreign-born. Those who were satisfied with their housing expressed a great deal of uncertainty toward urban renewal. Those who were dissatisfied were more likely to favour forced relocation for urban renewal. But a larger proportion of the dissatisfied also opposed relocation (32 % of the dissatisfied, versus 16 % of the satisfied). The latter trend disappeared however, when attitude toward forced relocation for freeways and apartments were examined. The foreign-born who expressed satisfaction with their present dwelling were significantly more negative toward forced relocation for those reasons. Uncertainty was higher for the dissatisfied.

TABLE 34. *Attitude to Forced Relocation for Urban Renewal by Housing Satisfaction, Foreign-born Only*

Housing Satisfaction	Favours Forced Relocation for Urban Renewal	"It depends"	Opposes Forced Relocation for Urban Renewal	Total
Satisfied %	38	13	49	100 (n=143)
Dissatisfied %	68	17	15	100 (n=41)
Total	45	14	41	100(N=184)

$\chi^2 = 16.44$, 2 d.f. $p < .001$; Cramèr's $V = 0.29$

Finally, it was expected that home-owners would be more integrated into the neighbourhood than renters and that the former would therefore be more opposed to forced relocation. However, no such relationship exists. Among renters, the amount of rent paid has virtually no effect on the attitudes of native-born respondents, and only a small, statistically non-significant effect on foreign-born residents. Among the latter, those paying high rents are slightly more favourable to the prospect of urban renewal.

Conclusion

In summary, we see some interesting patterns of differential attitude between the two sub-samples. While the native-born population was more positive toward the general notion of urban renewal activity, they tended to be extremely negative about the prospect of being forced to relocate for various reasons. While almost half of the native-born population apparently would not mind greatly being forced to move because of urban renewal, over eighty per cent of this population objected to being forced to move in order to build a school, new apartments, or a freeway or bridge. In comparison, while foreign-born respondents were somewhat more negative about urban renewal, less opposition was voiced to the prospect of being forced to move because of any of the other three above-mentioned activities. Again, however, a majority of the population in each case voiced negative opinions on these questions.

Possibly because of the relative homogeneity of the native-born population, most of the variables which we have tested have not been very significant predictors of attitude toward urban renewal for this population. By contrast, several of these variables have had some effect upon the foreign-born population, with the general pattern being that higher status individuals are more positive toward urban renewal. As well, the expression of satisfaction with dwelling and neighbourhood tended to produce negative reactions toward the prospect of being forced to move from the dwelling and/or neighbourhood. The generally negative response to the possibility of being forced to move from the area tends to further reinforce an interpretation of these urban renewal areas as relatively stable neighbourhoods, with populations by-and-large planning to remain in the area. Age, which in the case of the foreign-born, was closely associated with length of residence in Canada, proved to be the most consistent correlate of opposition to forced moves.

In the following chapter we shall consider whether the inhabitants of the areas surveyed were actively engaged in voluntary organizations and, if so, whether this was associated in any way with approval of, or opposition to, urban renewal. Differences between native and foreign-born householders in extent of social participation will also be considered as one aspect of immigrant integration.

VI

PARTICIPATION IN VOLUNTARY ASSOCIATIONS

Participation in community organizations has become highly relevant to urban renewal in Toronto. Neighbourhood improvement, rate-payers' and residents' associations have had important consequences for the way government and private urban renewal schemes can be implemented; citizen participation in the formulation of urban renewal plans seems to have gained a high degree of acceptance. Such participation can contribute to an effective urban renewal project. Indeed Rossi and Dentler (1961 : 292) conclude from their study of an urban renewal area in Chicago that

It seems likely that successful urban renewal in large cities—successful in the sense of widely accepted both within and without the neighbourhoods under renewal—will come primarily either in neighbourhoods that have indigeneous successful community organization or in neighbourhoods in which some outside agency manages to create one.

Because of the possibility of future urban renewal in the areas which have been studied here, it is relevant to investigate the extent of participation in voluntary associations, the types of organizations to which residents of these areas belong, and the differences between participants and non-participants in these areas.

Voluntary associations have been extensively studied by socio-logists, virtually from the inception of the discipline. Although the literature on voluntary associations discusses how important voluntary associations are in a democratic society, it also demon-strates clearly that participation is not uniformly distributed through-out the population. In fact, participation in voluntary associations is widespread only in middle and upper class groups of the popul-ation. Thus, the original perspective on voluntary associations can be qualified: most voluntary associations represent the middle and upper classes and their interests. Membership in voluntary associations is not a pattern of behaviour characteristic of working class people with the exception of labour unions and churches.

The dilemma which confronts those concerned with urban renewal is this: those who are most likely to be affected by urban renewal are least likely to organize effectively to express and promote their interests in the urban renewal process. Before any solution to this dilemma can come about it seems that an investigation of existing "organizational resources" in these urban renewal areas is in order.

The first section of this chapter discusses types of organizations in which membership is held. Labour unions and churches are treated separately. Four general areas are related to participation in voluntary associations other than church and union: first, social class; secondly, ethnicity; thirdly, integration; and finally, attitudes toward urban renewal.

No discussion of participation in voluntary associations can proceed without some consideration of the types of organization in which participation occurs. Eleven common types of membership were selected and participation is analyzed in these terms.

In previous research social class was found to be directly related to participation. Generally, as social class increases, participation increases. The relationship between ethnicity and participation is less well established. Previous research on the association of participation with native and foreign born status has been inconclusive.

An investigation of variables indicating integration, such as the neighbourhood integration score and satisfaction with house and job seems almost tautologous considering that participation in voluntary associations is itself indicative of integration. However, the concept of integration is often used without unequivocal definition in the literature. The fact that an individual participates in some major institutions of the society through voluntary associations does not necessarily imply that he is also highly integrated on a smaller-scale level such as a neighbourhood. Altogether it was found that 47 % of the sample claimed no organizational membership at all. There was no significant difference between native and foreign-born in this respect, but the former were more often members of two or more organizations.

Types of Organization: Overall Frequencies of Memberships

To what types of organizations do participants in urban renewal areas belong? How does this vary with birthplace and social class? Table 35 gives the raw figures for memberships in each organization, by birthplace and for the total population.

TABLE 35.   *Type of Organization by Birthplace*

Organization Type	Number of Memberships					
	Native-born		Foreign-born		Total	
	%	n	%	n	%	N
Labour Unions	28	(29)	50	(61)	41	(90)
Neighbourhood Improvement, Residents' and Ratepayers' Assoc.	1	(1)	2	(2)	1	(3)
Political Organizations	2	(2)	0	(0)	1	(2)
Lodges, Service Clubs, Veterans' Groups, etc.	7	(7)	3	(4)	5	(11)
P.T.A., Home and School	5	(5)	2	(2)	3	(7)
Youth Groups (as leader)	3	(3)	1	(1)	2	(4)
Church Groups	10	(10)	12	(15)	11	(25)
Community Centers	4	(4)	2	(2)	3	(6)
Social and Sports Clubs	25	(25)	11	(13)	17	(38)
Ethnic Organizations	4	(4)	14	(17)	9	(21)
Other	11	(11)	3	(4)	7	(15)
Total *	100	(101)	100	(121)	100	(222)

* The number of memberships exceeds the number of members since the latter sometimes belong to more than one organization.

The memberships that are held are distributed in a wide variety of organizations. The most widely held type of organizational membership is in labour unions. Social and sports clubs, church associated groups and ethnic organizations account for most of the other memberships. These latter organizations are all of the type which have been described as expressive in function rather than instrumental. That is, they cater to the expressive and socio-emotional needs of their members. Membership in instrumental groups such as neighbourhood improvement organizations, political organizations and PTA's is virtually negligible, as is membership in groups which are more mixed in function; that is, membership in instrumental-expressive groups such as lodges, service clubs, veterans' associations, and civic groups is also minimal. It is obvious, then, that in Toronto's urban renewal areas there is little in the way of membership in organizations that traditionally are means to influence the social environment. The type of voluntary association membership common in these areas does not have the function of giving the participants access to the power structure of the community.

Labour unions account for a much larger proportion of foreign-born than native-born memberships (50% vs. 29%). Otherwise, the only major difference lies in the category of social and sports clubs, which represent a greater proportion of native-born member-ships. However the foreign-born belong to ethnic organizations which often have goals and activities similar to those of the social clubs of the native born.

Labour Unions

The issue of whether labour unions are voluntary associations is critical in this research, since membership in labour unions occurred with such high frequency.

One of the main reasons why membership in labour unions is often not counted as a voluntary association membership is that the membership is usually a condition of employment, through closed shop and automatic check-off provisions in union contracts. Some data concerning the question of whether labour union mem-bership is voluntary are presented below. A non-compulsory union membership is one which is not required as a condition of employ-ment. Those memberships called compulsory are required, but a distinction is made between those members who say they would join the union regardless of the contract clause which requires them to join and those who would not join.

Overall, it can be concluded that labour unions are voluntary insofar as most members perceive their membership as something they would have done voluntarily. Only 14% of the union members felt they would not join the union unless it were compulsory. This is not to suggest that those who claim they would join their union regardless of requirements really would do so, but only to suggest that the pressure to join, through closed-shop practices, is not perceived in such a way as to make membership involuntary. Labour union members are required to do something that most of them want to do. Finally, although the differences between native-born and foreign-born union members are not large enough to be significant, there is a tendency for the native-born to be more committed to their labour unions, both through higher non-compulsory membership and through greater agreement with compulsory membership.

TABLE 36. *Type of Union Membership by Birthpaper, Labour Union Members Only*

Type of Union Membership	Native-born %	Foreign-born %	Total %
Non-compulsory membership	20	12	15
Compulsory, but respondent would join anyway	77	69	71
Compulsory, respondent would not join	3	19	14
Total	100(n = 30)	100(n = 57)	100(N = 87)

$\chi^2 = 4.59$, N.S.

If labour union membership is seen as a nonvoluntary activity, it would be expected that only the required conditions of membership would be fulfilled. In the case of unions, the paying of union dues is usually a requirement. However, attendance at meetings is not usually required except at times when the whole membership must vote, for example, on whether a new contract is acceptable. Table 37 below indicates, as was expected, that almost all union members pay dues. Of more interest is the finding that a strong majority of both native and foreign-born union members attend the meetings of their union, with the native-born slightly more active in this respect. The low proportion of union members in leadership positions is not surprising, simply because there are probably not a large number of leadership positions available. However, when attendance at meetings is used as an indicator, involvement in labour union affairs seems to be quite high.

If labour unions are, in fact, very close to voluntary associations from the point of view of most members, it may seem illogical to exclude unions from an analysis of community participation in general. This was done for two major reasons: the first lies in the basis of organization of trade unions; the second lies in the highly specific goals of trade unions.

TABLE 37. *Percentage Responding Positively to Questions about Labour Union Participation by Birthplace*

Labour Union Participation	Native-born %	Foreign-born %	Total %
Attendance at meetings	86	79	80
Financial contributions	93	95	94
Committee members	11	10	10
Executive members	7	2	3
Totals	N=28	N=59	N=87

Unions are organized on the basis of membership in a certain occupation or group of occupations. For this reason it is unlikely that unions would generate participation in the neighbourhood and community outside the particular occupation. In addition, the goals and activities of the labour union are specifically in the economic sphere and in the political sphere insofar as the latter applies to the economic interests of the union. That is, the unions become involved in the working conditions of their members; but the aspects of life outside of work, such as neighbourhood and community affairs, fall outside the sphere of union goals and activities. For these reasons, labour unions will be excluded from a definition of community organizations.

Religious Denomination, Religious Involvement, Ethnicity and Class

The literature on voluntary associations does not usually include church membership in its definitions of these groups. However, as mentioned in Chapter 2, while membership in a religious denomination may be non-voluntary, intense participation is voluntary in nature.

This section will examine first the relationship between religious denomination and ethnicity and religious denomination and class. Of course, the results are practically a foregone conclusion: given high levels of immigration from Southern Europe, a high proportion of the foreign-born are Roman Catholic. Table 38 shows the actual distribution.

TABLE 38. *Religious Denomination by Birthplace*

Religious Denomination	Native-born %	Foreign-born %	Total %
Roman Catholic	25	60	47
Protestant	61	18	34
Other	14	22	19
Total	100(n = 106)	100(n = 178)	100(N = 284)

$\chi^2 = 53.53$, 2 d.f $p < .001$;   Cramèr's $V = 0.43$

When religious denomination and class are examined, the coincidence of ethnicity and class produces a higher proportion of Roman Catholics in the blue-collar group. Over half of the blue-collar workers were Roman Catholic while only a third of the white-collar were. Among the native-born white-collar workers the proportion of Roman Catholics was only about one out of four.

However, of primary interest here is the degree of involvement in church activities of the respondents. Two factors were used to arrive at an index of religious involvement; the first is frequency of church attendance and the second is knowing the clergyman well. It seemed to the investigators that if a person knows the priest or minister of his church well, the implication is that he also participates intensively in the church. Furthermore, this item is very useful because it is applicable regardless of religious denomination.

Table 39 demonstrates the relationship between religious involvement and religious denomination.

TABLE 39. *Religious Involvement by Religious Denomination*

Religious Involvement	Roman Catholic %	Protestant %	Other %	Total %
High	30	10	11	20
Medium	33	22	6	24
Low	37	68	83	56
Total	100(n = 135)	100(n = 96)	100(n = 53)	100(N = 284)

$\chi^2 = 41.78$, 4 d.f. $p < .001$;   Cramèr's $V = 0,27$

Clearly, the Roman Catholic respondents were much more likely to be frequent church attenders and to know their clergyman. For slightly over two-thirds of the Protestants, religious adherence can be described as "nominal," whereas this is true of a little more than one-third of the Catholics. The very high proportion who had low religious involvement in the "other" category can be explained by the inclusion of atheists, agnostics and those with no religious affiliation in that category.

TABLE 40. *Religious Involvement by Birthplace*

Religious Involvement	Native-born %	Foreign-born %	Total %
High	11	25	20
Medium	19	27	24
Low	70	48	56
Total	100(n = 106)	100(n = 178)	100(N = 284)

$\chi^2 = 13.32$, 2 d.f. $p < .01 > .001$; Cramèr's $V = 0.32$

Seventy per cent of the native-born had low religious involvement, while 48% of the foreign-born did so. A quarter of the foreign-born had high religious involvement, as opposed to about a tenth of the native-born.

The effects of birthplace on religious involvement when denomination is controlled are indicated in Table 41. Although the differences are not statistically significant, a tendency for the foreign-born to have higher religious involvement does appear, both among Catholics and among Protestants.

TABLE 41. *Religious Involvement by Birthplace, Controlling for Denomination*

Religious Involvement	Catholic		Protestant	
	Native-born %	Foreign-born %	Native-born %	Foreign-born %
High and medium	52	65	27	44
Low	48	35	73	56
Total	100(n = 29)	100(n = 106)	100(n = 64)	100(n = 32)

$\chi^2 = 1.7$, N.S. $\chi^2 = 2.9$, N.S.

Occupational status had no effect on religious involvement. The white and blue-collar groups each had one-fifth high, and more than one-half low on religious involvement.

The next question approached is whether high religious involvement coincides with participation in other voluntary associations. Table 42 shows that those with high religious involvement were far more likely to be participants.

TABLE 42. *Participation by Religious Involvement*

Participation	Religious Involvement		
	High %	Medium and Low %	Total %
Participants	45	25	29
Non-participants	55	75	**71**
Total	100(n=56)	100(n=238)	100(N=294)

$\chi^2=8.32$, 1 d.f. $p<.01>.001$;   Phi$=0.17$

When birthplace was controlled, this relationship remained for both the native-born and the foreign-born. This finding is somewhat difficult to interpret since church-affiliated groups like choirs and Holy Name Societies were included as voluntary associations. Obviously, those with high religious involvement would be more likely to participate in church-affiliated groups. Thus the two variables tabulated are not independent of one another. Unfortunately the analysis necessary to answer the question of the types of organizations that those highly involved in churches belong to was not meaningful because of the small number of respondents.

When class was controlled, the relationship between religious involvement and participation described above appeared for the white-collar group. Eleven of the fifteen in that group were participants and high on religious involvement. However the proportions were almost reversed for those white-collar workers who were low or medium on religious involvement. In the blue-collar group, there was no significant difference between those high and those medium or low on religious involvement with respect to participation in other voluntary associations, although there was a greater tendency for those highly involved in religion to participate. These results are presented in Table 43.

TABLE 43.   *Participation by Religious Involvement Controlling for Occupational Status*

Participants	White Collar		Blue Collar	
	High Religious Involvement %	Low or Medium Religious Involvement %	High Religious Involvement %	Low or Medium Religious Involvement %
Participants	73	37	34	23
Non-participants	27	63	66	77
Total	100(n=15)	100(n=60)	100(n=41)	100(n=168)
	$\chi^2=6.55$, 1 d.f. $p<.02>.01$;		Phi$=0.29$ $\chi^2=2.34$, N.S.	

The conclusions to be drawn from the observations in this section are: first, that religious denomination is most highly related to religious involvement; that ethnicity is related to religious involvement mainly insofar as ethnicity is related to religious denomination; and that occupational status has no relationship to religious involvement. Finally, high religious involvement is positively related to participation in the white-collar group, but not in the blue-collar group.

Instrumental and Expressive Organizations and Leadership

Gordon and Babchuk (1959) developed a three-fold typology of organization derived from Parsonian theory.

Instrumental associations are those which have goals involving the wider society; that is, people outside the organization as well as those in it. This type has also been described as a social-influence organization. Expressive organizations typically serve the needs of their members only and do not involve those outside the organization. Social clubs, church-affiliated associations like choirs, or sports groups exemplify these. Instrumental-expressive organizations have a mixture of the two types of goals: they have some aspects of social influence groups and others of groups existing for the enjoyment of the members. Some examples are lodges and civic groups. The distribution of membership in these types of organizations is the focus of this section. As well, the characteristics of leaders are analyzed in these terms.

In Table 44 instrumental and instrumental-expressive organizations include the following: neighbourhood improvement, ratepayers' and residents' associations; lodges, service clubs, veterans' groups; P.T.A., Home and School; Youth Groups (as a leader). Expressive organizations are church groups, community centers, social and sports clubs and ethnic organizations.

TABLE 44. *Type of Organization by Birthplace*

Type of Organization	Native-born %	Foreign-born %	Total %
Instrumental and Instrumental-Expressive	30	15	22
Expressive	70	85	78
Total	100(n = 60)	100(n = 61)	100(N = 121)

$$\chi^2 = 3.67, \text{ N.S.}$$

Despite the lack of statistical signifance in Table 44, it suggests that the native-born may be somewhat more likely to belong to instrumental and instrumental-expressive organizations than the foreign-born, taking into account that the native-born are a smaller proportion of the sample (38% native-born, 62% foreign-born). In other words, the foreign-born are less likely to belong to groups which seek to influence the social environment than the native-born. These findings must, however, be cautiously interpreted since the trichotomy of organization types is inexact and significance was not established.

Type of organization membership did not vary strongly with occupational status. Surprisingly, there seems to be a higher rate of membership in instrumental and instrumental-expressive groups on the part of blue-collar workers.

Particularly relevant to an appraisal of organizational resources in urban renewal areas is a consideration of leadership. Leaders were defined as persons who either were members of committees of organizations or were executives. Labour unions were excluded from consideration.

TABLE 45. *Type of Organization by Occupational Status*

Type of Organization	White Collar %	Blue Collar %	Total %
Instrumental and Instrumental-Expressive	16	26	22
Expressive	84	74	78
Total	100(n = 38)	100(n = 65)	100(N = 103)

$$\chi^2 = 1.49, \text{ N.S.}$$

It was expected that white-collar respondents would be over-represented as leaders, but the results (Table 46) do not support the hypothesis strongly.

TABLE 46. *Leadership and Membership by Occupational Status*

Membership	White Collar %	Blue Collar %	Total %
Leaders	13	6	8
Members	31	19	22
Non-members	56	75	70
Total	100(n = 64)	100(n = 185)	100(N = 249)

$$\chi^2 \text{ invalid; expected frequency} < 5$$

Six per cent of the blue-collar group were leaders, while thirteen per cent of the white-collar group were. However, the raw figures were small: in our sample, there were eight white-collar and eleven blue-collar leaders. Thus more extensive analysis of leaders would not be fruitful with this sample. Incidentally, when leadership in labour unions is counted, the proportions of leaders increased to fifteen per cent of the white-collar groups and nine per cent of the blue-collar groups.

Roughly one in ten of the residents of urban renewal areas have some kind of leadership position. One might conclude from this that, from a point of view of organizing the area for purposes of participation in urban renewal plans, there would be a good pool of local leadership on which to draw. On the other hand, the question of whether leadership in expressive organizations involves the same abilities as leadership in instrumental organizations is an open question.

Social Class and Participation in Voluntary Associations*

Social class has been the best predictor of participation in voluntary associations in previous research on the subject.

The usual indices of social class are education, occupation and income. As well, Blishen (1967) has developed a system of scores indicating social class for a large number of occupations in Canada. This measure is based on a combination of occupation, education required for a specific occupation and income typical for a specific occupation.

The relationship between education and participation is readily apparent (see Table 47). In the group with low education, almost 80% were non-participants and only 8% were highly involved in voluntary associations. In the group with 9 to 11 years of education, the rate of participation almost doubled. In the group with 12 or more years of education, non-participation declined only slightly, to 58 % but high participation increased to almost 21 % of this group.

TABLE 47. *Participation by Education*

Extent of Participation	Years of Full-Time Education			
	8 Yrs. or Less %	9-11 Years %	12 Yrs. or Over %	Total %
None	79	61	58	70
Low	13	23	21	18
High	8	16	21	12
Total	100(n=164)	100(n=77)	100(n=67)	100(N=308)
	$\chi^2 = 14.51$, 4 d.f.	$p < .01$;	Cramèr's $V = 0.22$	

Participation similarly varies with occupational status. White-collar workers are much more likely to be participants and one-fifth of them are high participants. Of course, this one-fifth represents only 5% of the sample. Despite the important differences between the two groups it must be kept in mind that even in the white-collar group, less than half participate in any kind of voluntary association.

* Labour unions and churches are excluded from the definition of participation and all tables unless otherwise specified.

TABLE 48. *Participation by Occupational Status*

Extent of Participation	Blue Collar %	White Collar %	Total %
None	74	56	70
Low	16	24	18
High	10	20	12
Total	100(n = 209)	100(n = 75)	100(N = 284)

$\chi^2 = 9.70$, 2 d.f. $p < .01$;   Cramèr's $V = 0.18$

Income is less simply related to participation. Tables 49 and 50 present two types of income: the first is total family income; the second is family income divided by the number of wage-earners in the family.

TABLE 49. *Participation by Family Income*

| Extent of Participation | Income | | | |
	Less than $4000 %	$4000-8000 %	$8000+ %	Total %
None	67	76	53	69
Low	18	16	29	20
High	15	8	18	11
Total	100(n = 60)	100(n = 152)	100(n = 62)	100(N = 274)

$\chi^2 = 12.29$, 4 d.f. $p < .02$;   Cramèr's $V = 0.15$

The relationship between family income and extent of participation is not very strong. It appears that the middle income group has the lowest rate of participation. As expected, the highest income group had a high rate of participation. It is surprising that the lowest income group did not have a *lower* rate of participation. An analysis of this group by occupational status indicates that the higher rate of participation here was not produced by a substantial number of white-collar workers; there were only 5 of them in the low income group.

When the number of wage-earners in the family is taken into account in determining income, again no large difference emerge.

TABLE 50. *Participation by Average Income per Wage-earner*

| Extent of Participation | Average Income per Wage-earner | | | |
	Less than $4000 %	$4000-8000 %	$8000 and more %	Total %
None	75	66	63	70
Low	15	26	16	19
High	10	8	21	11
Total	100(n=149)	100(n=103)	100(n=51)	100(N=303)

$\chi^2=11.40$, 4 d.f. $p<.05$;   Cramèr's $V=0.14$

Non-participation varies inversely with income but the relationship is very weak. Some difference does appear between middle and upper income groups: the former are more likely to have low participation while the latter have more high participants. There is no difference between middle and low income groups with respect to high participation. The difference in these two groups is in the extent of low participation.

TABLE 51. *Participation by Blishen Score of Occupational Status*

| Extent of Participation | Blishen Score | | |
	Low (25.36-39.86) %	High (40.05-76.69) %	Total %
None	75	55	70
Low	15	27	18
High	10	18	12
Total	100(n=212)	100(n=73)	100(N=285)

$\chi^2=11.10$, 2 d.f. $p<.01$;   Cramèr's $V=0.17$

We can conclude that extent of participation is more highly related to educational level and occupational status than to income. In other words, an increase in income among blue-collar workers does not necessarily lead to a more middle-class life style as represented by participation. The relationship between the Blishen score of occupational status and participation again shows the direct effect of social class on participation. See Table 51.

Table 52 gives us some indication of the effect of social mobility on participation. Because of the way the data were coded, only upwardly mobile and downwardly mobile groups can be compared.

TABLE 52. *Participation by Social Mobility*

Extent of Participation	Mobility		
	Downward %	Upward %	Total %
Non-participants	74	66	70
Participants	26	34	30
Total	100(n = 113)	100(n = 124)	100(N = 237)
	$\chi^2 = 1.50$, N.S.		

The effect of stability is not known. The table indicates that the downwardly mobile have a lower rate of participation than the upwardly mobile. However, these effects are too small to be significant. The findings only suggest that mobile persons adopt the patterns of participation of their new status rather than maintaining their old.

One of the questions to which this study addressed itself was whether working class participants were differentiated from non-participants by their identification with the middle class, which could act as a reference group for them. Table 53 shows the relationship between participation and subjective social class identification. Apparently there is no significant difference between participants and non-participants, either blue-collar or white-collar, in this respect.

TABLE 53. *Participation by Subjective Social Class, Controlling for Occupational Status*

Extent of Participation	White Collar		Blue Collar	
	Middle Class %	Working Class %	Middle Class %	Working Class %
Non-participants	45	62	62	76
Participants	55	38	38	24
Total	100(n = 22)	100(n = 42)	100(n = 26)	100(n = 159)
	$\chi^2 = .99$, N.S.		$\chi^2 = 1.77$, N.S.	

Although 21% of the blue-collar participants described them-selves as middle class, opposed to 12% of the blue-collar non-participants this is not a significant difference.

Table 54 explores the aspirations of blue-collar respondents toward higher social status. Participants are more likely to reject aspirations to a higher social status than non-participants are. It is, of course, difficult to draw a conclusion about this finding, since the possibility exists that the blue-collar participants who claim low aspiration for higher status are simply being defensive. On the other hand, if these results are taken at face value, it seems that there may be no necessary connection between being middle class, (or having middle class reference groups) and participation. Other aspects of working class life must be at the basis of low working class participation.

TABLE 54. *Participation by Aspiration to Higher Satus,*
Blue Collar only

Extent of Participation	Aspiration to Higher Status	Indifferent, or No Aspiration to Higher Status	Total
	%	%	%
Non-participants	85	65	74
Participants	15	35	26
Total	100(n=89)	100(n=106)	100(N=195)
	$\chi^2 = 10.46$, 1 d.f. $p < .01$; Phi=0.23		

Compared to the participants, the non-participants have relatively high aspiration to middle class status. In addition, these people are more likely to subscribe to middle class values. Table 55 tabulates agreement and disagreement with the statement "A university education is always better than a good trade." The participants were less likely to agree with this than the non-participants. It is suggested that the reason for these differences can be found in one of the basic themes of the literature on participation: namely, that voluntary associations are integrative for the participants. That is, the working class participant is more highly integrated not only

TABLE 55. *Attitude toward Education by Participation, Blue Collar Only*

Extent of Participation		Feels University is Superior to Trade	Feels University is not Superior, or Indifferent	Total
Participants	%	77	23	100 (n = 149)
Non-participants	%	60	40	100 (n = 53)
Total	%	73	27	100(N = 202)

$$\chi^2 = 5.57, \ 1 \ \text{d.f.} \quad p < .02; \quad \text{Phi} = 0.17$$

in the whole society but particularly is more satisfied with his perceived social status.

Finally, it is important to note that the strong relationship between participation in voluntary associations and social class depends on the exclusion of labour unions from the definition of voluntary association. This fact is well-demonstrated by Table 56 which corresponds to Table 47 above except that labour union participation is included in the former.

TABLE 56. *Participation (including Labour Union) by Education*

Extent of Participation	Years of Education			
	8 years or less %	9-11 years %	12 or more %	Total %
None	57	52	45	53
Low	26	19	31	26
High	17	29	24	21
Total	100(n = 164)	100(n = 77)	100(n = 67)	100(N = 308)

$$\chi^2 = 6.78, \ \text{N.S.}$$

First of all, the inclusion of labour union memberships raises the levels of participation in all groups, but especially in the one with the lowest level of education. In addition, the differences between the educational levels are not large enough to be significant. The same results were found when participation with labour union included was tabulated against occupational status and the Blishen score.

These findings emphasize the theoretical importance of labour unions in participation research. The decision in this research has been to exclude labour unions from community organizations for the reasons specified earlier. However, research on participation with other underlying goals might have given rise to the opposite decision. One of the aims of further research should be to clarify the meaning of participation in labour unions both empirically and theoretically. This process would also be highly useful for other types of voluntary associations.

Ethnicity and Participation

The tables relating indicators of social class and participation in voluntary associations other than church and unions have clearly established that the latter varies directly with the former, as had been noted in almost all previous research. As mentioned above, the relationship between participation and ethnicity is less well known. From one point of view, lower rates of participation may be expected because the immigrant may be less well integrated into the community. Not only may the idea of participation be strange to him, but also he may be handicapped by such factors as inadequate knowledge of the language. On the other hand, if there is any well established ethnic subculture which includes voluntary associations, he may be well integrated in it and have some degree of participation in the ethnic "community." Table 57 compares the rates of participation of native-born and foreign-born respondents.

TABLE 57. *Participation by Birthplace*

Extent of Participation	Native-born %	Foreign-born %	Total %
None	63	75	70
Low	20	16	18
High	17	9	12
Total	100(n=120)	100(n=196)	100(N=316)

$\chi^2=6.27$, 2d.f. $p<.05>.02$;   Cramèr's $V=0.14$

The native-born do tend to have a higher level of participation than the foreign-born, but the result is only marginally significant.

However, if social class as reflected by occupational status is controlled, this slight relationship between birthplace and extent of participation increases; that is, differences between blue-collar native-born and foreign-born become statistically significant at the 2 % level only.

TABLE 58. *Participation by Birthplace, controlling for Occupational Status*

Extent of Participation	White Collar		Blue Collar	
	Canada %	Other %	Canada %	Other %
None	48	65	69	77
Low	32	15	19	17
High	20	20	12	6
Total	100(n=41)	100(n=34)	100(n=65)	100(n=144)

$\chi^2=3.07$, N.S. $\chi^2=8.64$, 2 d.f. $p<.02$ Cramèr's $V=0.20$

Although they suggest that foreign-born are less likely to participate regardless of occupational status, the differences in Table 58 do not allow the rejection of the null hypothesis that there is no difference between native-born and foreign-born in rates of participation when occupational status is controlled. Similarly when class as indicated by the Blishen Score is controlled, no significant differences between native-born and foreign-born emerge. Nevertheless, the tendency is greater for both middle and working class native-born to be participants with the greatest difference in the blue-collar group.

TABLE 59. *Participation by Birthplace controlling for Blishen Score of Occupational Status*

Extent of Participation	High		Low	
	Canada %	Other %	Canada %	Other %
None	49	60	69	79
Low	31	24	14	15
High	20	16	17	6
Total	100(n=35)	100(n=38)	100(n=72)	100(n=140)

$\chi^2=1.06$, N.S. $\chi^2=5.60$, N.S.

It is possible that the small differences between native-born and foreign-born stem from the fact that many foreign-born respondents have been in the country long enough to become sufficiently assimilated to adopt Canadian patterns of participation.

Because of low cell frequencies in the category of high participation, only participation and non-participation are used as the independent variables in Table 60 which investigates the effect of period of immigration and participation. The results, which are not significant, proceed in the expected direction: the longer an immigrant has been in this country, the more likely he is to participate, even though participation is relatively low in all streams of immigrants.

TABLE 60. *Participation by Period of Immigration, Foreign-born Only*

Participation	Before 1950 %	1950- 1960 %	1961- 1965 %	1966 or later %	Total %
Non- participants	68	72	76	81	74
Participants	32	28	24	19	26
Total	100	100	100	100	100
	(n=31)	(n=74)	(n=41)	(n=48)	(N=194)

$$\chi^2 = 2.22, \text{ N.S.}$$

There does seem to be a relationship between an immigrant's subjective identification as Canadian and participation, although the direction of causality is not established. The answers to the question "Do you feel now that you are fully a Canadian or do you still feel as if you belong more in your old country?" are presented in Table 61. Those who identify themselves as Canadian have slightly higher rates of participation than those who retain feelings of belonging to their country of origin. This difference continues to exist for high and low degrees of participation. Of course, as mentioned above, it is not known whether participation increases because of feeling Canadian or whether feeling Canadian increases because of participation.

In conclusion, it would be rash to suggest that ethnicity has *no* effect on participation. However, it is safe to conclude that social

TABLE 61. *Participation and Ethnic Identification, Immigrants Only*

Extent of Participation	Feels wholly Canadian %	Feels partly or wholly Foreign %	Total %
None	64	81	73
Low	22	12	17
High	14	7	10
Total	100(n = 80)	100(n = 105)	100(N = 185)

$\chi^2 = 6.94$, 2 d.f. $p < .05 > .02$;   Cramèr's $V = 0.19$

class is a much more important factor in accounting for rates of participation in the areas under study here.

In addition, it is apparent that participation among foreign-born may be related to their identification with Canada. Of course this does not necessarily conflict with membership in such groups as ethnic organizations and maintenance of some aspects of the culture of the country of origin.

Integration and Satisfaction

If voluntary associations promote integration into society for the individual we would expect that participants have higher scores on such items as the neighbourhood integration scale and on satisfaction with home and work. On the other hand, some voluntary associations specifically serve to voice the discontent of their members. In that case, lower scores on the indices of integration would be expected. The following table explores the relationship between neighbourhood integration and participation.

TABLE 62. *Participation by Neighbourhood Integration*

Extent of Participation	Neighbourhood Integration		
	Low %	High %	Total %
None	71	69	70
Low	19	19	19
High	10	12	11
Total	100(n = 182)	100(n = 102)	100(N = 284)

$\chi^2 = 0.29$, N.S.

There is no significant difference between participants and non-participants in neighbourhood integration. In addition, Table 63 demonstrates that satisfaction with housing, neighbourhood, job and schools does not vary with participation. A combined score based on satisfaction with housing, neighbourhood, job and school was calculated and averaged to a five point scale.

TABLE 63. *Combined Satisfaction Score by Participation*

Participation		Combined Satisfaction Score		
		(1-3)	(4-5)	Total
Non-participants	%	20	80	100(n = 199)
Participants	%	25	75	100(n = 85)
Total	%	21	79	100(N = 284)

$$\chi^2 = 0.38, \text{ N.S.}$$

Finally, it is most surprising that participation was not strongly related to lengths of residence. Previous research had suggested that cutting points of less than one year, one to two years and more than two years would reveal a curvilinear relationship with participation, with the middle category forming a peak of participation. Low cell frequencies in the first two categories of length of residence allowed the analysis only on the basis of neighbourhood and address. Most of those in the category of "less than one year" were short-distance migrants; they had moved within Metro or within the neighbourhood. What the non-significant differences in

TABLE 64. *Participation by Length of Residence in Neighbourhood*

Participation	Length of Residence			
	Less than 1 year %	1 - 2 years %	More than 2 years %	Total %
Participants	29	20	31	29
Non-participants	71	80	69	71
Total	100(n = 35)	100(n = 44)	100(n = 200)	100(N = 279)

$$\chi^2 = 2.01, \text{ N.S.}$$

TABLE 65. *Participation by Length of Residence at Address*

Participation	Length of Residence			
	Less than 1 year %	1 - 2 years %	More than 2 years %	Total %
Participants	30	22	32	30
Non-participants	70	78	68	70
Total	100(n = 67)	100(n = 49)	100(n = 163)	100(N = 279)

$$\chi^2 = 1.80, \text{ N.S.}$$

these two tables suggest is that short-distance migrants maintain memberships in their old areas, which they gradually drop. Then participation is low until new associations are joined.

In order to observe the relationship between length of residence and participation for the long distance migrants, cutting points with a larger range were used (see Table 66). None of the differences are significant but are in the expected direction. That is, one would expect that with increased length of residence, greater integration with the surrounding society would occur, partly through participation. What is surprising is that the differences are not larger.

Although the functions of voluntary associations are integrative, this does not lead necessarily to higher levels of satisfaction or a greater attachment to neighbourhood. Participants in these areas resemble non-participants in these respects. Also, there should be further research on the relationship of length of residence to participation, particularly to discover the extent to which membership in voluntary associations are "portable"; that is, the extent to which membership in organization is maintained despite geographical relocation.

Attitudes Toward Urban Renewal and Participation

The final section in this report deals with attitudes toward urban renewal as the dependent variable and participation as the independent variable.

TABLE 66. *Participation by Length of Residence at various Geographical Levels*

Location	Length of Residence	Participants %	Non-participants %	Total % N
Canada	3 yrs or less	19	81	100(48)
	4 - 8 years	28	72	100(40)
	9 yrs or more	33	67	100(194)
	Total	30	70	100(282)
Ontario	3 yrs or less	19	81	100(53)
	4 - 8 years	22	78	100(50)
	9 yrs or more	35	65	100(178)
	Total	30	70	100(281)
Metro	3 yrs or less	22	78	100(59)
	4 - 8 years	25	75	100(59)
	9 yrs or more	34	66	100(164)
	Total	30	70	100(282)
Neighbourhood	3 yrs or less	24	76	100(100)
	4 - 8 years	25	75	100(64)
	9 yrs or more	37	63	100(114)
	Total	29	71	100(278)
Address	3 yrs or less	28	72	100(44)
	4 - 8 years	27	73	100(64)
	9 yrs or more	35	65	100(71)
	Total	30	70	100(279)

First, do participants differ from non-participants in the extent to which they favour or oppose urban renewal? Table 67 demonstrates that there is no difference in attitude toward urban

TABLE 67. *Attitude to Urban Renewal by Participation*

Attitude to Urban Renewal	Participants %	Non-participants %	Total %
In favour	67	66	66
Indifferent or opposed	33	34	34
Total	100(n=81)	100(n=175)	100(N=256)

$$\chi^2 = 0.04, \text{ N.S.}$$

renewal for participants and non-participants. Furthermore, no differences emerged when occupational status was controlled.

Table 68 shows that the majority of the white-collar group is favourable to moving because of urban renewal. The blue-collar group was less favourable. In addition, blue-collar participants and non-participants show significant differences in their attitude: the difference is not so much in the favourable-unfavourable categories but rather in neutrality on the subject. Only four per cent of the blue-collar participants were neutral, while seventeen per cent of the non-participants were. In addition, the blue-collar participants were somewhat more likely to be favourable toward the idea of a forced move than blue-collar non-participants.

TABLE 68.   *Attitude toward Moving because of Urban Renewal by Participation, controlling for Occupational Status*

Attitude to Forced Move	White Collar		Blue Collar	
	Participants %	Non-Participants %	Participants %	Non-Participants %
Favourable	63	70	48	39
Neutral	14	15	4	17
Unfavourable	23	15	48	44
Total	100(n=33)	100(n=39)	100(n=50)	100(n=150)
	$\chi^2=0.12$, N.S.		$\chi^2=5.35$, N.S.	

The white-collar participants and non-participants varied in their acceptance of forced relocation for various specific facilities although no significant differences appeared for the blue-collar group. In addition, blue-collar and white-collar participants showed significant differences.

A pattern which has been mentioned in an earlier chapter of this report continued to appear: all respondents favoured forced relocation for schools over forced relocation for a freeway; the latter was favoured over forced relocation for highrise apartments.

Tables 69 to 71 show the main differences in acceptance of forced relocation. Consistently, the white-collar participants are more likely to find forced relocation acceptable. The group which consistently finds forced relocation least acceptable is the white-collar non-participants, followed by the blue-collar non-participants and then the blue-collar participants. Participants are generally more in favour of forced relocation than non-participants, although this difference is never significant for the blue-collar groups. It is most interesting to note that these differences in attitude seem to be more related to participation than to class. Tables 72 and 73 show that a tabulation of occupational status and attitude toward forced relocation for schools does not produce significant differences, while one of participation and attitude to forced relocation does.

TABLE 69. *Attitude to Forced Relocation for School and Participation controlling for Occupational Status*

Attitude to Forced Relocation	White Collar		Blue Collar	
	Participants %	Non-Participants %	Participants %	Non-Participants %
Favourable	42	19	29	36
"It depends"	37	22	29	18
Unfavourable	21	59	42	46
Total	100(n=33)	100(n=41)	100(n=52)	100(n=149)

$\chi^2=10.65$, 2 d.f. $p<.01>.001$; Cramèr's $V=0.38$ $\chi^2=2.83$, N.S.

TABLE 70. *Attitude to Forced Relocation for Freeway by Participation, controlling for Occupational Status*

Attitude to Forced Relocation	White Collar		Blue Collar	
	Participants %	Non-Participants %	Participants %	Non-Participants %
Favourable	36	20	28	29
"It depends"	40	19	26	17
Unfavourable	24	61	46	54
Total	100(n=33)	100(n=41)	100(n=50)	100(n=150)

$\chi^2=10.00$, 2 d.f. $p<.01>.001$; Cramèr's $V=0.37$ $\chi^2=1.86$, N.S.

The implication of Tables 70 to 72 is that opposition to forced relocation lies in the relatively unorganized groups of this area and white collar participants are the least and white collar non-participants the most opposed.

TABLE 71. *Attitude to Forced Relocation for Highrise by Participation, controlling for Occupational Status*

Attitude to Forced Relocation	White Collar		Blue Collar	
	Participants %	Non-Participants %	Participants %	Non-Participants %
Favourable	30	20	25	23
"It depends"	24	12	21	16
Unfavourable	46	68	54	61
Total	100(n=33)	100(n=40)	100(n=52)	100(n=150)
	$\chi^2=3.71$, N.S.		$\chi^2=.83$, N.S.	

TABLE 72. *Attitude to Forced Relocation for Schools by Occupational Status*

Attitude to Forced Relocation	White Collar %	Blue Collar %	Total %
Favourable	30	34	33
"It depends"	28	21	23
Unfavourable	42	45	44
Total	100(n=73)	100(n=202)	100(N=275)
		$\chi^2=1.77$, N.S.	

TABLE 73. *Attitude to Forced Relocation for Schools by Participation*

Attitude to Forced Relocation	Participants %	Non-participants %	Total %
Favourable	34	33	33
"It depends"	32	19	23
Unfavourable	34	48	44
Total	100(n=85)	100(n=190)	100(N=275)
	$\chi^2=8.48$, 2 d.f. $p<.02>.01$; Cramèr's $V=0.17$		

Conclusion

Presented here is a summary of the empirical findings on participation in voluntary associations. A discussion of these findings in the context of other research is reserved for the concluding chapter.

First, participation varies with social class as measured by level of education, occupational status and the Blishen score. Income is less directly connected with participation.

Secondly, when social class as measured by occupational status is controlled, there is little difference in the rate of participation of native-born and foreign-born respondents. Foreign-born are more likely to be participants if they identify with Canada.

Thirdly, neighbourhood integration, levels of satisfaction and length of residence are not strongly related to participation.

Fourthly, labour union membership is very high. Other memberships tend to be in organizations with expressive rather than instrumental goals. Leadership is not concentrated by class as much as by birthplace.

Finally, participants and non-participants differ in their attitudes toward urban renewal and forced relocation with white-collar participants slightly more favourable than others.

VII

CONCLUSION

In this final chapter an attempt will be made to place the findings of the study in the broader perspective of sociological theory. We shall also examine some sources of intra-population variation arising from the concentration of particular ethnic groups in certain neighbourhoods. In conclusion, the principal results of the study will be summarised. These will focus on the two related questions of immigrant integration and future urban re-development in certain central city districts.

Following his studies in Chicago some fifty years ago, Robert Park suggested a cycle in the relations between immigrants and the receiving society, commencing with an initial stage of contact giving rise to competition and conflict. (Park and Burgess, 1921.) It was assumed that the latter phase would be followed, in due course, by a period of "accommodation" in which the conflict would be contained by various mechanisms including the partial segregation of different ethnic groups from each other. He believed that, eventually, minorities would be completely assimilated into the receiving population. More recent researches and advances in sociological theory have cast doubts upon the appropriateness of this model of immigrant absorption in advanced industrial and post-industrial societies. (Richmond, 1969.) In particular it cannot be assumed that a process of complete "assimilation" leading to the disappearance of distinctive ethnic minorities is inevitable. Under certain conditions a stable pluralistic system may emerge with or without accompanying ethnic stratification.

Also using a "conflict" model of the social system of metropolitan areas John Rex more recently considered some sociological aspects of the "zones of transition" which serve as immigrant reception areas in modern cities (Rex, 1967; 1968). Adequate housing at a price people can afford is a "scarce resource" in most large cities. When this is the case the population may be represented in terms of several "housing classes" competing in the market. In contemporary urban societies the market situation is not determined exclusively by economic factors. A political element has been introduced through the exercise of planning authority and zoning regulations, the enforcement of housing standards, including controls over multiple occupation, overcrowding etc., government influence upon mortgage lending and interest rates, rent controls and subsidies, the increasing importance of public housing and the intervention of various levels of government in the urban renewal process. Under these conditions recent immigrants and some other ethnic minorities may find themselves disadvantaged relative to the indigenous population and established immigrants.

Rex admits that his analysis of the situation in Birmingham, England, is influenced by the particular historical circumstances of industrial development in Britain during the nineteenth and early twentieth centuries. His model also assumes the exercise of political power by organised working-class interests through municipal councils and the allocation of public or "council" houses. In this respect it should be noted that approximately a quarter of the total housing stock in England and Wales, and a rather larger proportion in the Birmingham area studied by Rex, is subsidised public housing. In contrast, in Metropolitan Toronto in 1972 only three percent of the housing stock was publicly owned and administered. Furthermore, the rapid growth of Metropolitan Toronto in the last twenty-five years in terms of population has coincided with a construction boom. Only recently has the demand for accommodation begun to exceed the supply of available housing. In 1968 there were 5,000 names on the waiting list for public housing, but by 1971 this had risen to approximately 20,000. In the first three months of 1972 the Ontario Housing Corporation housed 1,042 applicants but received 3,815 new applications. The most serious housing shortage is for large families. Since the majority of units available through the public housing authorities are of the two—or three—bedroom type they are of little use to larger immigrant families, even if the latter were interested in such accommodation. Allocation to public housing is based upon a "points" system of tenant selection. Although ethnic origin or immigrant status are not explicitly taken into account, the length of residence qualification and the points allocated for veteran status give some advantage to native-born Canadians. At the same time many immigrants show a clear preference for home ownership when this becomes economically feasible, rather than rented accommodation whether private or public.

One of the objectives of the present study was to ascertain whether the central city districts of Toronto designated as "long term improvement areas" were functioning as "zones of transition". Such a zone of transition generally includes, as well as recently arrived immigrants of low education and economic status, internal migrants from rural areas, transients, social isolates and deviants of all sorts including prostitutes, drug addicts and alcoholics. Such an area is usually quite heterogeneous from an ethnic point of view and characterised by low cost housing, cheap lodging houses, bars, cafés and welfare agencies. The outstanding characteristics of such transient areas are a high rate of population turnover, relative lack of social organisation, a high incidence of petty crime due to lack of family and community controls, combined with severe psychological stresses generated by the need to adapt to an alien environment. Such a neighbourhood or zone performs important adaptive and integrative functions for those who pass through it, enabling them to obtain essential food, shelter and human companionship until such time as the newcomers are sufficiently acculturated and economically successful to move on to more socially acceptable localities and stable social relations. However, some people may settle more or less permanently in such an area, where they are sheltered from the greater competition and pressure for conformity characteristic of the wider society.

Often a transient reception area continues to perform such functions for generation after generation of recently arrived migrants from rural and other areas in the same country, or abroad. However, under certain conditions such a neighbourhood may be converted into either a ghetto or the ecological focal point of an ethnic social network. A ghetto is most likely to occur when a migrant group finds its way out blocked by prejudice and discrimination. This is particularly liable to happen when the group in question is highly visible due to particular racial characteristics.

It will tend to grow numerically until few members of other groups are left. At the same time the ghetto will tend to develop social institutions and attitudes among its members that are a form of accommodation to discrimination. The ghetto leaves its mark upon the personality of its inhabitants and the situation frequently gives rise to violence. (Clark, 1965.)

Some degree of ethnic residential segregation may also come about voluntarily and be result of deliberate choice on the part of individuals and families who wish to avail themselves of opportunities for social intercourse, recreation, religious observance, education and consumer behaviour, using ethnic institutions that happen to be convenient. (Richmond, 1972.) However, increasing facilities of communication by telephone and ease of transportation by automobile have rendered the preservation of ethnic ties less dependent than they were formerly upon living close together. In Montreal it has been shown that a high degree of institutional completeness of an ethnic community is a more important determinant of whether a person will have the majority of his social relations with others of his own ethnic group, than the degree of residential segregation. (Breton, 1961.) It is significant that in the urban renewal areas of Toronto thirty percent of householders said that most of the people they knew well were living in the same neighbourhood (that is within five blocks), but sixty-three percent said that most of the people they knew well belonged to the same ethnic group. Furthermore, comparatively few householders belonged to ethnic organizations or participated in any local community association. Therefore, the term "ethnic community" should be used with some reservation. It is probably more appropriate to speak of extended social networks which are not necessarily confined to the immediate neighbourhood, although the presence of relatives and friends in the immediate locality may contribute to neighbourhood integration.

Generally speaking, the evidence from the survey did *not* support the view that the central city areas concerned were serving as "zones of transition", although some neighbourhoods may have performed such a function at one time. As measured by past moves and future plans to move, the population of these areas appeared to be at least as stable as those in other parts of Metropolitan Toronto. In fact, it is probably necessary to think in terms of geographical mobility and relatively high rate of population turnover as "normal" phenomena in the present and future development of large metropolitan areas. Possibly due to the rapid rate of growth and high proportion of immigrants, mobility is undoubtedly one of the characteristics of householders in Toronto. In 1970, approximately half of all heads of households in Metropolitan Toronto were foreign born, four out of every five of whom had entered Canada since the end of World War II. Half of all heads of household in Metropolitan Toronto in 1970 had moved at least once within Toronto during the preceding five years. (Richmond, 1972.)

The householders covered in the urban renewal survey represented, after weighting, approximately 8 % of all households in Metropolitan Toronto, 25 % of households in the City Municipality and one third of all households in the inner part of the city. These were the, approximately, 50,000 households included in the 1966 Metropolitan Toronto Planning Board's Urban Renewal Report, excluding areas A and H which were outside the City boundaries. The six areas covered were not contiguous nor were they homogeneous from the point of view of housing and social conditions or ethnic composition. Unfortunately, the size of the sample did not permit a detailed examination of the local variations. However,

TABLE 74. *Household Heads by Birthplace and Area of Residence*

Birthplace	Area of Residence			
	B & C %	D & F %	F & G %	TOTAL %
Canada	35	28	54	38
Britain & Ireland	9	3	10	6
Italy	34	14	6	17
Portugal	1	31	0	13
Poland & U.S.S.R.	6	7	1	5
All other countries*	15	17	29	21
	100 (n=82)	100 (n=133)	100 (n=101)	100(N=316)
	$\chi^2=114.6$, 22 d.f., $p<.0001$; Cramèr's $V=0.43$			

* including Germany, Netherlands, Greece, U.S.A. and others.

by grouping the areas into three adjacent pairs and comparing these in the light of information from survey and other sources it is possible to distinguish certain distinctive features. The distribution of householders by birthplace and area is shown in Table 74.

AREA AND ETHNIC DIFFERENCES

Areas F and G

Areas F and G to the east of Yonge Street include the neighbourhoods where the most extensive public redevelopment has taken place in the past. The proportion of native-born Canadians was about average for Metropolitan Toronto and was 54 % of all householders at the time of the survey. This part of Toronto tended to serve as a reception area for internal migrants from other parts of Canada, particularly the rural areas of northern Ontario, Quebec and the Maritimes. Of the foreign-born, those born in Britain, Greece and Asian countries were numerically predominant. Although excluded from the sample survey, the Regent Park and Moss Park public housing projects are located in this part of Toronto. These rehousing schemes are the outcome of earlier urban renewal efforts in the city in which some of the oldest working class housing was cleared.

Also located within areas F and G were several current urban renewal areas that have been subject to considerable controversy. These include the Trefann, Don Mount and Don Vale neighbourhoods. The original intentions of planners and politicians in these areas appears to have been to undertake extensive demolition with a view to redevelopment at higher densities and with superior quality housing that would increase the local tax base. However, local residents' associations developed sufficient political influence to pressure City authorities into abandoning these early plans for expropriation in favour of rehabilitation and the maintenance of the distinctiveness of these localiites. Although the sample survey showed that active participation in neighbourhood associations was rare, the asociations in question had open membership and, as far as possible, were run on democratic lines. However, they were not without opposition from rival groups claiming to represent property owners, residents and neighbours. The latter tended to be run more autocratically but nevertheless had a voice at City Hall. (Lorimer, 1970.) Disputes over the plans for urban renewal in these areas have been going on for almost a decade during which time only the minimum housing standards and safety regulations have been maintained. As a consequence housing conditions and local amenities have further deteriorated. Until 1968 it was assumed that the Federal and Provincial levels of government would provide significant financial assistance toward any urban renewal plan that was eventually agreed upon. However, in that year the Federal Government froze all funds for urban renewal throughout the country. As a consequence no further developments have taken place to date, although new legislation is expected. Meanwhile, private developers have been assembling land in some neighbour-hoods east of Yonge Street and have proceeded with schemes involving extensive demolition and the building of highrise apart-ments or the rehabilitation of older houses and their sale as middle-class "town houses". In many cases these developments have required political support in the form of revised zoning by-laws. These have also generated protests from local residents supported by a minority of the City Councillors. (Nowlan and Nowlan, 1972.)

In the light of the experience of Trefann Court, Don Vale and Don Mount areas it was not surprising to find that the householders in areas F and G were more likely than those elsewhere to be actively opposed to urban renewal. However, there was no signi-ficant difference between these two areas and others in the survey in the degree of attachment to the neighbourhood, as measured by the neighbourhood integration score, or in frequency with which they would object to being forced to move as a consequence of urban renewal. Residents of these areas, as in the other neigh-bourhoods studied, tended to view the locality in which they lived in terms of its convenience and cheapness rather than in terms of any sentimental attachment. In this connection it is interesting to note that James Lorimer, in his intensive participant observation of residents living in one of the urban renewal areas east of Parliament Street, should have noted that many of the inhabitants think wist-fully about living on a farm in the country and regard the suburbs as a compromise between the central city and the country. The young couples that Lorimer knew thought that, if they could afford it, they would be better off living in the suburbs than in the city.

"Long-term residents east of Parliament seem more attached to the area and more conscious of its qualities, but even they express their feelings as a hard-headed weighting of advantages versus disadvantages . . . . They have none of the romantic enthusiasms which outsiders sometimes affect for the 'colour-ful', 'intensive' life of neighbourhoods like east of Parliament." (Lorimer, 1971, p. 113.)

The survey lent quantitative support to this qualitative impression.

Areas D and E

Areas D and E were west of Yonge Street and mainly south of Bloor Street. These areas differed in a number of important res-pects from those east of Yonge Street. Contained within area E is Alexandra Park Public Housing Project which is the outcome of an earlier "slum clearance" programme. Adjacent to Alexandra Park is the Kensington Urban Renewal Area which has also been given priority for further development although no specific plans have been implemented so far. The focal point is the Kensington Market which has long served as a cosmopolitan street market reflecting the ethnic composition of wave after wave of recently arrived immigrants. Before the First World War it was a Jewish market and was later diversified by Polish, Ukrainian and other immigrants. The most recent groups to settle in the area and utilize the market are the Portuguese and the West Indian immi-grants. Original development plans called for the complete clearance of the open street market and the building of new facilities with adequate parking and other improvements. However, the Ken-sington Area Residents Association resisted such sweeping plans and proposed a more conservative rehabilitation of the market and the surrounding residential properties. Leadership in the Association was provided by social workers connected with the local Community Centre and by some long-term residents. How-ever, participation by recent immigrants appears to have been minimal. In any case the moratorium on urban renewal following the freezing of federal funds has meant that no major improvements have been implemented so far.

The residents of the Alexandra Park Public Housing Project were excluded from the sample. The remaining householders in areas D and E included a very high proportion of recently arrived immigrants. Only 28 % of those in the sample were born in Canada. The largest single nationality was the Portuguese who constituted 31 % of the householders. Slavic-speaking, mainly Ukrainian, householders were the second most important ethnic group in the area constituting 14 % of householders. They were generally longer term residents.

The Slavic population is found mainly in the south-western part of this area. An earlier study examined the feasibility of housing rehabilitation in this area which corresponded closely with the Gore Vale District. (Rose, 1966.) It was pointed out that nearly 90 % of the homeowners sampled in that area were elderly immigrants to Canada who had resided there at least from the end of the Second World War if not earlier. The majority had discharged accumulated mortgage debt and were reluctant to incur further debts to fulfil rehabilitation objectives. The homeowners in this district were described as "a stable, conservative, determined set of homeowners who are wary and suspicious of public and voluntary action towards urban renewal."

Within area D is another distinctive district known as the "Lower Ward", corresponding with census tracts 49 and 63 to the south. This neighbourhood probably corresponded more closely to a classic "zone of transition" than any other included in the survey. The population is extremely heterogeneous although the Portuguese are beginning to outnumber other groups. Housing conditions are poorer than elsewhere and lodging houses catering for single males are common.

The social system of the "Lower Ward", as it was more than a decade ago, has been vividly described by W. E. Mann. He described the neighbourhood as probably the least desirable residential section of Toronto. Adjacent to railway tracks and truck depots the air is heavily polluted and the side streets jammed with heavy trucks. His analysis focussed on the "old Canadians" of British origin who were already a minority, constituting only about one third of the population in 1961. Since then the proportion of native-born Canadians of British origin has been further reduced by death and out-migration. Those that remain exhibit the same characteristics observed by Mann in the late 1950's. He considered that the low social status, bleak physical appearance, residential and social instability tended to attract native-born families with lower education, poor physical health and unstable personalities. The "old Canadians" tended to segregate themselves from the European immigrants but they were also cut off socially from higher status English Canadians. Living in the Lower Ward carried with it the stigma of a slum dweller. The native-born residents depended heavily upon their own extended kinship group in the neighbourhood, where family authority tended to be matri-archal. The many local bars provided the main source of psycho-logical support and primary group attachments for the local male population. Adolescent gangs performed socialisation functions and gave security to the young people growing up in this economically and culturally deprived neighbourhood. (Mann, 1961.)

Since Mann's study of the "Lower Ward" the proportion of immigrants in the area has increased. In particular, there is a growing Portuguese population that is beginning to put down roots. In contrast with the native-born residents of the area the Portuguese tend to be young, energetic, hard working and ambitious. They are not locked into the cycle of depression and apathy described by Mann. Potentially they are upwardly mobile. A journalistic description of recent changes in the "Lower Ward" drew attention to the large number of Portuguese homeowners who were rehabili-tating the property in the area without the assistance of any government subsidies. The Portuguese were described as a "free-lance slum clearance movement". (Villiers, 1971.) In this con-nection it is interesting that the sample survey showed overall that foreign-born homeowners planned to spent an average of $467 on improvements to their own homes in the subsequent twelve months compared to an average of $387 by native-born home-owners. The latter figure was influenced by a few people who planned to spend a great deal and a majority who planned to spend nothing or very little.* Furthermore, the foreign-born Italian and Portuguese were very often employed in the construction industry. They would be most likely to use their own labour and to obtain materials cheaply. It seems that areas D and E were in the process of transformation from a "zone of transition" into a relatively stable immigrant neighbourhood with fairly well established Slavic

---

* If those planning to spend nothing are excluded the figures are $1,100 and $856, respectively.

and Portuguese populations. As in other parts of Toronto the residents of these areas did not necessarily consider themselves to be permanently settled in the neigbourhood. If suitable opportunities arose they would be willing to improve their material conditions by moving elsewhere. Meanwhile, local ethnic institutions and the presence of relatives provided valuable social support. The most serious conflict is likely to arise if the local authority were to enforce zoning regulations since a large part of this area is eventually scheduled for non-residential purposes. There was no significant difference between the residents of areas D and E in their degree of attachment to the neighbourhood as measured by the neighbourhood integration score. However there was a statistically significant tendency for the residents of these areas, particularly the Portuguese, to be positively in favour of urban renewal even when this involved forced removal for purposes of building free-ways, apartments, schools etc.* It was originally hypothesized that residents in a "zone of transition" would be less attached to the neighbourhood and therefore less opposed to urban renewal. If the areas in which the Portuguese have settled are regarded as approximating to a "zone of transition", this hypothesis was only partially supported. Opposition to being forced to move and high neighbourhood integration were strongest among respondents with low education and, when the effect of low education is partialled out, the association between Portuguese mother tongue and these variables ceases to be significant.

Areas B and C

Areas B and C were to the north and west of the central city. On several indicators they were intermediate between the areas to the east of Yonge Street and those south of Bloor Street. Thirty-five percent of the householders were Canadian born and the largest single immigrant group was the Italian which constituted 34 % of the households. Immigrants living in these areas had

---

* As one Portuguese speaking interviewer undertook all the interviews with Portuguese immigrants the possibility of interviewer bias influencing some of the responses of this group cannot be completely excluded, although there is no positive evidence to support such an interpretation of their somewhat a-typical replies.

resided longer in Canada and had more friends outside the immediate neighbourhood. Housing conditions were generally better
than in the other areas studied.

Residents of areas B and C were less likely than those elsewhere
to be informed of any plans for residential clearance or demolition
in their neighbourhood. This is not surprising since these were
not regarded as priority areas by either the City or the Metropolitan Toronto Planning Boards. Home ownership was particularly
characteristic of residents of these areas, as only 44 % of householders were renting accommodation compared with an average of
53 % in the study as a whole. Multiple occupation was characteristic
of 44 % of households. Although this was about average for the
urban renewal areas as a whole it was considerably above the proportion in areas F and G (35 %) and below that in areas D and
E (62 %). There was no significant difference between areas B
and C and the others in the neighbourhood integration score or
in the probability of support for opposition to urban renewal and
forced relocation.

However, when the Italian speaking population was examined
separately certain important differences emerged. A little over
half the Italian population surveyed resided in areas B and C.
Generally speaking, Italian householders were more likely to be
homeowners, to have relatives in the neighbourhood and to have
no plans to move. They scored significantly higher than average
on the neighbourhood integration score. Unlike the Portuguese
they were not significantly more favourable toward urban renewal
but neither were they as likely to be opposed to forced relocation
as often as those of British origin. The Italian households living
in these areas were more established than the Portuguese but were
not as economically successful as those who had moved out of
the city toward the Italian neighbourhoods in suburbs such as
North York. Although Italian immigrants in suburbs were likely
to maintain close contact with relatives and friends, many of
whom live in the same neighbourhood, the degree of ethnic concentration was less than in the city. Italian households in suburban
areas had often moved there from the central city districts included
in the urban renewal survey. Those who moved north tended to
have resided longer in Canada, to be acculturated and fluent in
English and better integrated economically. (Ziegler, 1972.)

IMPLICATIONS FOR URBAN RENEWAL POLICIES

The areas covered in the present survey were those designated by the Metropolitan Toronto Planning Board as potential urban renewal areas. Only a few selected neighbourhoods were currently subject to specific plans for expropriation or rehabilitation and even these plans were temporarily suspended. The suspension was partly due to the unwillingness of the federal government to participate financially in the schemes but was also a consequence of the lack of agreement between local neighbourhood associations and the planning authorities. While researches elsewhere have been undertaken immediately before or after an ongoing urban renewal scheme, this study focusses on the poorer central city districts of Toronto in what might be termed the pre-planning stage. In many cases definite plans have not been drawn up and renewal schemes will probably not be implemented for a number of years. In the light of the present study it is possible to anticipate some of the problems that may be generated at that stage.

The potential urban renewal neighbourhoods studied were ethnically heterogeneous with an above average proportion of immigrants and native-born in-migrants from rural areas. The average level of education and economic status was low. Households were predominantly working class, stable residentially and marked by a high level of satisfaction with neighbourhood and dwelling. Generally speaking, the areas studied were not "zones of transition" serving as reception areas for migrants who would leave as soon as they could afford to do so. Selected districts appeared to have performed this function in the past but there was an increasing tendency for the foreign-born inhabitants to purchase houses and to rehabilitate them at their own expense. At the same time, they built up extensive networks of kith and kin and made use of a variety of ethnic institutions in the neighbourhood. Although many people had plans to move the proportion who did so was not higher than the average for Metropolitan Toronto as a whole.

The householders in these areas were generally favourable towards the idea of urban renewal, when seen as an opportunity to improve the quality of housing and local amenities. There was rather greater opposition in principle to forced moves resulting from the building of freeways, apartments or schools. However, the majority of residents were not entirely opposed to the possibility of moving, as a consequence of urban renewal, under certain conditions. In the event of expropriation, homeowners favoured sufficiently generous compensation to enable them to purchase comparable accommodation elsewhere. Those renting accommodation considered that they should be assisted to find alternate accommodation at similar or lower rents. Some favoured public housing while others were more disposed toward the idea of subsidized rents. Where the rehabilitation of existing houses is envisaged, financial assistance towards meeting higher housing standards would be required in many cases. Given the low income of many of the householders only limited improvements could be expected without subsidy, although immigrants were more inclined to undertake such work than others.

Very few of the residents in the areas surveyed were active participants in local residents' associations. Even in those localities where urban renewal plans had been prepared, and about which there was considerable political controversy, there was some doubt concerning the representativeness of the neighbourhood associations concerned. In many cases initiative and leadership had depended on a small minority of local professional and business people. Nevertheless, serious misunderstandings and problems of communication, as well as conflicts of interest appeared to have arisen in the negotiations with the City. (Cross, 1972.) It is evident that such problems are likely to be even more serious in the event of urban renewal plans being drawn up for those areas with a high proportion of immigrants, many of whom have only a limited knowledge of English.

The study of participation in voluntary organizations indicated that labour unions, churches and social clubs were the most frequent types of association to which people in these areas belonged and that there were many people who did not participate in any voluntary associations of this kind. None of these organizations appeared to be well adapted to cope with the problems likely to arise in the event of urban renewal. In his study of an Italian neigbourhood in Boston, Herbert Gans showed that not until the city's schemes were about to be implemented did the local residents recognize the threat to their community and attempt any organized resistance or protest. (Gans, 1962.) The present study suggests that much the same situation could arise in Toronto. A combination of low education and a lack of political consciousness or effective power at the local level could result in the needs and interests of local inhabitants being subordinated to those of developers and politicians, concerned more with the economic than the social factors in urban change. (cf., Lorimer, 1970, 1971.)

The survey showed that the highest degree of neighbourhood integration and the maximum resistance to being forced to move because of urban renewal was likely to come from the *older* residents of the neighbourhoods concerned. Even after the effects of education, length of residence and ethnicity were partialled out, age continued to be the factor most highly correlated with opposition to urban renewal and forced relocation. No other basis of social differentiation showed as such a persistant correlation. The finding is understandable in the light of the generally more conservative attitude of older people, the longer period of residence in the neighbourhood and greater probability of home ownership. These attitudes were probably further affected by the realistic knowledge of the constraints upon future geographic and social mobility compared with the aspirations of younger householders. Given the increasing pressure upon housing as a scarce resource in Toronto, and the rising costs of houses to purchase or rent, older people would feel more threatened by urban renewal activities. Even when urban renewal was interpreted as rehabilitation the cost of such work might be beyond the means of older people and involve drawing upon savings that they planned to use on retirement. Therefore, any plans for urban renewal in the future should be particularly sensitive to the special needs, interests and problems of older people, irrespective of ethnic background.

IMMIGRANT INTEGRATION

This study has focussed only upon a particular segment of the immigrant population of Metropolitan Toronto. Generally speaking the foreign-born residents of the areas studied were more recent arrivals, less well educated and of lower economic status than immigrants in other parts of Toronto. A measure of "non-neighbourhood integration" was used to ascertain the use made of and participation in facilities in other parts of the City as well as further afield in Metropolitan Toronto and other parts of Ontario.* A subsequent survey has shown that 65 % of all householders in Metropolitan Toronto scored six or more on this scale. A third of all Italian householders in Metropolitan Toronto scored six or more on this scale, compared with only 23 % of the householders, both Canadian and foreign born, in the urban renewal areas. Whereas only 8 % of all householders in Metropolitan Toronto scored 3 or less, 33 % of those in the urban renewal areas did so. Although there was a greater tendency for the foreign born, particularly the Portuguese, to score low on this measure of integration there was a marked tendency for native-born householders also to be much less integrated, by this measure, than people living elsewhere in Metropolitan Toronto. One of the implications of this is that both native and foreign-born householders in the potential urban renewal areas were likely to be more dependent upon local services and amenities, as well as their own primary social networks.

The evidence reviewed earlier in this report showed that the foreign-born heads of household were more likely to be in manual and service occupations than the native-born but that there was no significant difference in the distribution of family income. Immigrants were more likely to be home owners, to be in multiple occupation of dwellings and to experience greater overcrowding than native-born householders. Nevertheless, satisfaction with housing and neighbourhood was high. Immigrants showed a marked preference for living close to relatives and made extensive use of ethnic shopping and other facilities. There was no significant difference between the native and foreign-born in the intention to move from neighbourhood but the foreign-born showed a slightly greater degree of attachment to the neighbourhood as measured by the neighbourhood integration score. However, this difference

---

* The question on which this scale was based was as follows: "Here is a list of places you can visit and things you can do. Have you ever been to High Park, Toronto Island, Canadian National Exhibition, Royal Ontario Museum, O'Keefe Centre, Toronto Symphony Orchestra Concert, Niagara Falls, Algonquin Park?" Respondents scored from zero to eight according to the number of affirmative responses.

appears to have been due largely to the lower level of education of the foreign-born and the difference ceased to be significant when this was partialled out. In fact, among immigrants, middle or old age and low education appeared to be the most important determinants of high neighbourhood integration.

The examination of social participation and membership of voluntary organizations showed that the foreign-born householders were more often members of Labour unions than the native-born. The foreign-born were also active in church groups, social and sports clubs as well as ethnic organizations. Largely as a consequence of low education and social class position combined with shorter period of residence, the foreign-born householders scored lower on the Chapin scale of social participation when labour unions were excluded from calculation, but there was no significant difference when they were included.

The relationships between birthplace, ethnicity, area of residence and the various indicators of attitude toward urban renewal and immigrant integration are effectively summarized in the correlation matrix shown in Table 75. The relatively poor integration of those of Portuguese mother tongue may be attributed to their low education and recency of arrival in Canada. In contrast, it seems that those of Slavic and Italian mother tongue have made significant progress in the process of cultural and social integration into Canadian society. In this connection it is important to keep in mind the essentially pluralistic character of Canada and of Metropolitan Toronto in particular. (Richmond, 1969.)

Although not exhibiting many of the characteristics associated with high economic success and middle-class social status the immigrants in the urban renewal areas surveyed appeared to be successfully integrating themselves into local, working-class and ethnic sub-cultures in which their own goals were being effectively achieved. This was evidenced by the high level of satisfaction expressed by the immigrant respondents as far as housing, neighbourhood and jobs were concerned. Presumably due to a sense of relative gratification compared with conditions in their former country the Portuguese immigrants, who objectively were in the poorest housing and lowest economic status, were significantly more satisfied than the other residents of the areas studied. However, this does not preclude the probability that as the foreign-born residents of these potential urban renewal areas get older, become more acculturated and identify with Canadian norms and values, conflicts which are now only latent will become more evident and may manifest themselves in opposition to official plans. In particular, the enforcement of zoning regulations, destruction of residential areas or recreational amenities in anticipation of freeway extensions, the rehabilitation of houses by the enforcement of standards beyond the means of existing inhabitants, together with the spot clearance of pockets of poor housing in certain neighbourhoods could all contribute to overt conflicts of interest. Although not grounded in any objective ethnic differences, such conflicts could acquire ethnic overtones due to the residential concentration of particular nationalities. Needless to say, intelligent planning and due regard for the needs and interests of local inhabitants regardless of ethnic origin could reduce such conflict, but experience of urban redevelopment in Toronto to date does not give ground for optimism in this respect. (Lorimer, 1970; Granatstein, 1972).